NOSH
VEGETARIAN
MEAT-FREE & DOWN-TO-EARTH

OTHER COOKBOOKS IN THE NOSH SERIES BY JOY MAY

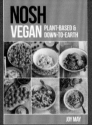

ISBN: 9780993260971

ISBN: 9780993260964

ISBN: 9780956746450

ISBN: 9780956746498

ISBN: 9780993260919

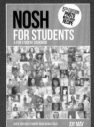

ISBN: 9780993260933

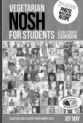

ISBN: 9780993260940

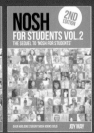

ISBN: 9780956746405

ISBN: 9780956746481

ISBN: 9780993260957

} @NOSHBOOKS

CONTENTS

LETTER FROM JOY

I love cooking and have been writing cookbooks for the last 19 years. For every new book I write with my family, we start by trying to get into the minds and lives of those we are writing for. This process never fails to be a fascinating one for us, as we seek to delve into what makes people 'tick'.

Although we have a popular vegetarian student book, I have still received countless requests for a mainstream vegetarian cookbook. Early in 2019 I released 'NOSH Vegan' and now here is its twin, 'NOSH Vegetarian'.

Full disclosure: if you look at my other books, you will see that I am not a 'signed-up' vegetarian. However, that does not mean I don't love veg. One of my rather random and particular loves is beetroot: raw, roasted, pickled, sliced, grated, blitzed, or whole. However it comes, it is a winner for me. So please induldge me, as I have included quite a few beetroot recipes in this book.

Seriously though, we know that eating vegetarian is a very healthy choice, but it also needs to be enjoyable. Eating the same old things over and over again is not much fun and won't produce a heathy diet either. There is plenty of variety here to keep your taste buds guessing, so...

...enjoy.

WHO HAVE WE WRITTEN THIS BOOK FOR?

Gone are the days when vegetarian books were bought solely by 'dyed-in-the-wool' vegetarians. The once niche topic of eating meat-free has been transformed into mainstream.

With that in mind, who have we written this book for?

NEWBIES

You might be new to all of this stuff. For one reason or another, be it ethical or health, you find you are in the position of calling yourself a vegetarian for the first time, but you haven't got a clue where to start. We aim to make our recipes as accessible as possible and not filled with crazy ingredients that you can only get in farmers' markets, or 'boutique' delis.

TOE-DIPPERS

OK, let's be honest, you might have no intention of giving up your favourite, bacon sandwich any time soon. However, you can't ignore all of the research showing how eating so much meat is damaging both our planet and our bodies. Something has to change. Your start might simply be to add a few meat-free dishes into your weekly menu. Hopefully, we will make that transition just that little bit more delicious!

OLD-TIMERS

You didn't think we were going to forget about you guys did you? None of this stuff is new to you. If fact, you have been telling us all for years that we need to take a long, hard look at our life choices when it comes to eating meat. We want to thank you for campaigning with your message on animal welfare, global warming and health. As a token of our gratitude, here are some new recipes to boost your repertoire.

DAIRY

Eating a 'plant-based' diet brings a huge amount of benefit. As vegetarians also choose to eat eggs and dairy, they are readily able to access nutrients, such as B12 and amino acids, not available, or not easily found, in plants alone. We would encourage you, in choosing to eat eggs and dairy, to select humane and healthy sources.

Where possible, we try to buy organic dairy from grass-fed cows and free-range, organic eggs. Personally, we also use 'raw milk', that is neither pasteurised nor homogenised. It comes with all of its' natural goodness, including the healthy bacteria that is great for our guts. It also tastes amazing! We appreciate that raw milk is not available in supermarkets, but can often be obtained from local farms.

SUGAR

Where recipes in this book require sweetness, we seek to avoid using processed, refined sugar. Again, personally, we use 'raw honey' (only heated up to 42°C and hence not pasteurised), pure, maple syrup and organic, raw, coconut sugar. The reason for this is that refined sugar has been stripped of its natural nutrients, leaving only pure calories with no benefits, apart from a quick burst of energy that we may never use! We have sought to use the most suitable, unprocessed sugars, 'packaged' naturally with vitamins, fibres, antioxidants and minerals. These give all of us the amazing health-benefits, together with a slow release of sugar into our systems, rather than the 'sugar-spikes' we get from highly-processed sugars.

In the 'sweet' section, there are a few deviations from the above, where the ingredients struggle to 'hold together' when using unrefined sugars. We would suggest these are not part of your everyday diet!

WHY VEG?

Like many people, you may want to increase your intake of fruit and veg. But why?

ANIMAL WELFARE

There have been so many documentaries which show us how badly some animals in the food industry are treated. It seems, collectively, we have reached a 'tipping point' and we can't ignore such things anymore.

THE ENVIRONMENTAL IMPACT

Although all of us can't ignore this, there are all sorts of conflicting stats out there about the carbon footprints of certain food-types, one recent report by 30 nutrition scientists from around the world concluded that, to meet the food challenge of a growing world population, meat and sugar consumption, at a global level, should drop by 50% by 2050.

HEALTH

If we eat a good, balanced, vegetarian diet then this will give us a very healthy approach to eating. The heart is protected when we eat high-fibre whole grains and legumes that keep our blood sugar levels steady and also when we eat nuts with their low glycemic index, fibre, protein and healthy fatty acids. Studies have shown the positive impact on cancer levels, cholesterol levels, the incidence of type 2 diabetes and lower body weight, as a result of eating vegetarian.

MONEY

We received an email today from one of our readers looking to switch to a more vegetarian-based diet to save money. We really hope that this book helps with that. To help, each recipe is priced-up with an average of Sainsbury's and Tesco pricing. It is much easier to save money eating vegetarian, without cutting the quality of the ingredients we buy. In this context, however, we would still recommend that you buy as much organic produce as your finances permit. Our bodies were not made to handle all the pesticides and fertilisers that might be present in our food. Money spent on good quality food is a good deal!

NUTRITION

RDA'S

You will see that we have put the nutrition figures at the bottom of each recipe, including a bar-chart showing percentage of the official recommended daily allowance (RDA). These RDA's are, in fact, figures applicable to women, so should be adjusted for men and children.

FATS

Plant-based diets sometimes struggle to achieve a good balance of fats, but, for vegetarians, this is made easier by incorporating dairy and eggs into the mix. Saturated fat, monounsaturated fat and polyunsaturated fat all occur naturally, and should be included in a balanced diet. 'Trans fat', on the other hand, is unnatural, a byproduct of industrial fat production, and should be avoided. The three good fats above don't necessarily make us 'fat', as is commonly assumed, but they do have a high calorie-count per gram, so consume wisely.

Personally, we are not afraid of higher saturated-fat meals when they come from good, natural products, such as grass-fed dairy, free-range eggs and organic coconut products. Saturated fat forms the foundation of the body's cell membranes and has been shown to increase HDL cholesterol in the body (the good cholesterol).

We encourage you to do your own research, so that you feel comfortable on this subject.

VEGAN AND GLUTEN-FREE

Throughout this book we highlight vegan and gluten-free recipes/options. Based on this, 97% of the recipes are suitable for those who are gluten-free and 32% of the recipes are suitable for vegans. We hope this helps.

THE FAMOUS MUG

This actual mug is the same one I used when writing 'NOSH for Students' back in 2000. It has a place in my heart. Although now cracked in several places, it still has a special spot in our mug cupboard!

If you are new to NOSH Books, then you may not have cooked with mug measures before, but give it a go, it's so much simpler. What is quicker than just grabbing a mug and filling it? What is easier to remember than a 'mug of this', or '2 mugs of that'?

This mug holds $\frac{1}{2}$ a pint, or 300ml of liquid, and is the exact size of the mug pictured opposite. So, find a mug that measures up to this one and you won't go far wrong. If you love your scales and measuring jugs, we have still added the weights and volumes for you, so don't worry.

This mug has been used by over half a million people, so it's a bit bashed up! That may not be completely true, but this book marks a milestone for the the NOSH family, of over 500,000 books being sold. That's a lot of people using a mug, ditching the scales and grabbing a little cooking freedom.

THIS MUG HOLDS
½ A PINT OR 300ML

ACTUAL SIZE

YOUR FREE NOSH BOOKS APP

To help you plan and shop for your food, we have designed a free app to create menus and shopping lists. Simply browse any of our books and add recipes of your choice to a weekly menu. Then the app does all the tedious work of creating the shopping list for you and boom! You are ready to shop.

No more aimless wandering around the supermarket, only to get home and still not be able to make a meal. What have you got to lose? Download it for FREE.

AUBERGINE

It might seem a littl...
how we have done h...
actually to make su...

GLUTEN-FREE OPTION: us...

5 medium **potatoes** thinly sliced

2 tablespoons **olive**

2 **aubergines**, sliced into 4 lengthways

2 **eggs**

4 slices **bread**

20g **butter**, measur... using packet

2 **spring onions**, chopped

1 stick **celery**, chop...

2 tablespoons **horseradish sauce**

12 **cherry tomatoes** chopped

WILD RICE WITH SPINACH AND CASHEWS

Nutty wild rice, nutty cashew nuts, I'm really surprised that the word 'nutty' doesn't actually feature in the title of this recipe. Maybe we should change that in the future.

GLUTEN-FREE OPTION: use GF stock cubes.

¾ mug (190g) **mixed wild rice**

2 tablespoons **olive oil**

1 **red onion**, chopped

2 **carrots**, grated

2 cloves **garlic**, finely chopped

125g **mushrooms**, sliced

½ mug (150ml) **water**

1 **veg stock cube**

2 tablespoons **tomato purée**

1 teaspoon **cumin**

1 teaspoon **ground coriander**

200g **spinach**, roughly chopped

½ mug (100g) **cashew nuts**

1 Put the rice in a saucepan with 2 mugs of boiling water. Bring to the boil and simmer gently, with a lid on the pan, for 25 minutes.

2 10 minutes before the rice is cooked, heat the oil in a wok or large frying pan. Add the onion, carrots and garlic. Fry until things begin to brown.

3 Add the mushrooms, water, stock cube, tomato purée, cumin and coriander. Season well with salt and pepper. Bring to the boil and then turn down to simmer for 5 minutes.

4 Add the cooked rice to the pan along with the spinach and cashews. The spinach will wilt.

86

88

BANANA PANCAKES

There are quite a few ingredients to these pancakes, but they are totally worth the content.

GLUTEN-FREE OPTION: use GF oat bran, flour and baking powder.

PANCAKES

1 ripe **banana**, mashed
4 tablespoons **Greek yogurt**
3 tablespoons **buttermilk**
1 tablespoon **coconut sugar**
2 teaspoons **vanilla extract**
1 **egg**
3 tablespoons **oat bran**
5 tablespoons **plain flour**
1 teaspoon **baking powder**
½ teaspoon **cinnamon**

4 tablespoons **coconut oil**
200g **fresh raspberries**
maple syrup

1 Put the banana, yogurt, buttermilk, coconut sugar, vanilla extract and egg in a large bowl and mix well, but don't beat.

2 Add the rest of the pancake ingredients and mix well.

3 Heat some of the coconut oil in a frying pan. Add tablespoons of the mixture and fry on a low heat until golden brown on both sides. The mixture should make 8 small pancakes. You will need to fry in batches.

4 Serve with raspberries and maple syrup.

RDA 100%

   GF OPTION Ve OPTION

RAISIN AND APRICOT GRANOLA

We love making our own granola, it is so quick and easy to make. You can play around with different types of dried fruit if you like. See page 7 for our approach to sugar.

VEGAN OPTION: use maple syrup instead of honey and serve with dairy-free yogurt/milk.

GLUTEN-FREE OPTION: use GF oats.

4 tablespoons (60ml) **maple syrup**

2 tablespoons **coconut oil**

2 tablespoons **water**

4 tablespoons (90g) **honey**

2 mugs (200g) **oats**

½ mug (100g) **cashew nuts**, chopped

1 mug (100g) **flaked almonds**

1 ½ mugs (75g) **flaked coconut chips**

¾ mug (75g) **desiccated coconut**

⅓ mug (80g) **raisins**

½ mug (80g) **ready-to-eat, dried apricots**, chopped

1 Preheat the oven to 170°C fan/190°C/gas 5. Grease a large roasting tray.

2 Put the maple syrup, coconut oil, water and honey in a small saucepan and gently heat until the coconut oil melts. Remove from the heat.

3 Mix the oats, cashews, almonds, flaked coconut and desiccated coconut in a large bowl. Add the contents of the saucepan and mix thoroughly.

4 Spread out on the roasting tray. Bake in the oven for 10 minutes. Take out of the oven and stir. Spread out again. Return to the oven for another 10 minutes, or until things just start to brown.

5 Remove from the oven, add the raisins and apricots, and stir.

6 Leave to completely cool before storing in a sealed jar.

RDA 100%

288kcal	6g	20g	10g	31g	13g	5g	0.05g
CALORIES	PROTEIN	FAT	SAT FAT	CARBS	SUGAR	FIBRE	SALT

£ 1.91 /PERSON · SERVES 2 · EASE ★★☆☆☆ · PREP 20 MINS · GF OPTION

SMASHED AVOCADO ON TOAST

Such simple and clean flavours with the richness of the egg and extra crunch from the coconut crisps. If you make a batch of the coconut crisps, they will keep for weeks in an airtight jar.

GLUTEN-FREE OPTION: use GF bread.

---

2 **avocados**

juice of ½ **lemon**

1 tablespoon freshly chopped **basil**

2 **spring onions**, chopped

4 **eggs**

4 slices **crusty bread/ sourdough**

butter

coconut crisps (see p216)

1 Peel the avocados, place in a bowl and squish with a fork. Season with salt and pepper.

2 Add the lemon juice, basil and spring onions.

3 Poach the eggs.

4 Toast the bread and butter it.

5 Spread the avocado on the toast, with the poached eggs on top.

6 Sprinkle over with coconut crisps.

RDA 100%

652kcal CALORIES	28g PROTEIN	42g FAT	15g SAT FAT	51g CARBS	4g SUGAR	7g FIBRE	2g SALT

PEANUT PORRIDGE

Turbo charge your porridge with peanut butter and chopped hazelnuts. You can use different nut butters if you wish.

VEGAN OPTION: use almond milk, or similar, instead of milk.

GLUTEN-FREE OPTION: use GF oats.

---

1 mug (100g) **oats**

2 mugs (600ml) **milk**

2 tablespoons **peanut butter** (see p218)

2 **bananas**, sliced

1 tablespoon **maple syrup**

2 tablespoons **roasted, chopped hazelnuts**

1 Put the oats, milk and peanut butter in a small saucepan and bring to the boil. Simmer for 1 minute.

2 Serve with bananas, syrup and hazelnuts.

RDA 100%

462kcal	24g	23g	6g	79g	45g	8g	0.5g
CALORIES	PROTEIN	FAT	SAT FAT	CARBS	SUGAR	FIBRE	SALT

BREAKFAST HASH

It is well worth making extra coconut crisps, so that you always have some on hand to add to simple recipes like this. You can buy coconut flakes online at Healthy Supplies or Ocado, or at Morrisons.

2 medium **potatoes**, cut into chunks

3 **sweet potatoes**, peeled and cut into chunks

3 tablespoons **coconut oil**

1 **red onion**, sliced

100g **kale**, chopped

4 **eggs**

coconut crisps (see p216)

1 Put the potatoes in a pan of boiling water. Simmer for 8 minutes and then drain.

2 Heat the oil in a wok, or large frying pan. Add the onions and fry for 2 minutes. Add the potatoes, season well with salt and pepper, and fry until the potatoes are browned.

3 Add the kale and fry for a further 3-4 minutes.

4 Poach or fry the eggs.

5 Serve with coconut crisps on top.

RDA 100%

| 477kcal | 14g | 21g | 15g | 60g | 15g | 8g | 1g |
| CALORIES | PROTEIN | FAT | SAT FAT | CARBS | SUGAR | FIBRE | SALT |

SERIOUSLY GREEN SOUP

You really can't get away from how green this soup is. I mean, just look at it!! Not only green, but full of great nutrition.

GLUTEN-FREE OPTION: use GF stock cubes.

1 tablespoon **olive oil**

1 **onion**, sliced

2 cloves **garlic**, chopped

2 tablespoons freshly grated **ginger**

200g **kale**

2 **veg stock cubes**

3 mugs (900ml) **almond milk**

½ mug (100g) **cashew nuts**

100g **spinach**

1 Put the oil in a large saucepan or wok. Add the onions and garlic and fry for 3 minutes.

2 Add the ginger and fry for 1 minute.

3 Add the kale, stock cubes and almond milk and bring to the boil. Simmer, with a lid on the pan, for 5 minutes.

4 Meanwhile, put the cashews in a dry frying pan and toast until browned. Remove from the pan and set to one side.

5 Add the spinach to the saucepan and simmer for a further minute. Season well with salt and pepper.

6 Blend the soup with a hand-held blender. Serve with the cashews.

RDA 100%

363kcal	13g	27g	4g	14	6g	6g	0.5g
CALORIES	PROTEIN	FAT	SAT FAT	CARBS	SUGAR	FIBRE	SALT

STILTON AND CAULIFLOWER SOUP

The tanginess of the Stilton really cuts through the creaminess of the cauliflour.

GLUTEN-FREE OPTION: use GF stock cubes and bread.

25g **butter**, measure using packet

2 **leeks**, sliced

2 cloves **garlic**, chopped

1 **cauliflower** cut into florets

2 mugs (600ml) **water**

2 **veg stock cubes**

100ml **double cream**

150g **Stilton cheese**, crumbled

2 tablespoons freshly chopped **chives**

bread to serve

1 Heat the butter in a large saucepan. Fry the leeks and garlic for 2 minutes.

2 Add the cauliflower, water and stock cubes. Season well with salt and pepper. Bring to the boil and simmer for 10 minutes.

3 Blitz with a hand-held blender until smooth.

4 Add the cream and half of the Stilton and bring to the boil.

5 Take off the heat and stir in half the chives.

6 Serve with the rest of the chives and Stilton sprinkled over.

RDA 100%

604kcal	23g	33g	20g	56g	9g	4g	2g
CALORIES	PROTEIN	FAT	SAT FAT	CARBS	SUGAR	FIBRE	SALT

£ 1.28 /PERSON | SERVES 4 | EASE ★★☆☆☆ | PREP 25 MINS | GF OPTION

EGG AND CHIVE MAYO ON SOURDOUGH TOAST

The red onions in this are transformed by being slightly pickled in the cider vinegar.

GLUTEN-FREE OPTION: use GF sourdough.

8 **eggs**

1 **red onion**, very thinly sliced

2 tablespoons **cider vinegar**

2 tablespoons **extra virgin olive oil**

2 tablespoons **maple syrup**

bag **lamb's lettuce**

3 tablespoons **mayo**

3 tablespoons freshly chopped **chives**

4 slices **sourdough bread**

coconut crisps (see p216)

1 Put the eggs in a pan of boiling water and simmer for 10 minutes. Drain the cooked eggs and rinse with cold water. Set to one side.

2 Meanwhile, place the red onion in a bowl, with the cider vinegar, and allow to stand for 5 minutes.

3 Mix the onion together with the olive oil and maple syrup. Add the lamb's lettuce and season well with salt and pepper.

4 Peel the shell from the cooled eggs and roughly chop. Add the mayo and chives and mix.

5 Toast the sourdough.

6 Divide the salad ingredients and egg mixture between the slices.

7 Sprinkle with coconut crisps.

RDA 100%

| 507kcal | 23g | 37g | 10g | 33g | 8g | 3g | 2g |
| CALORIES | PROTEIN | FAT | SAT FAT | CARBS | SUGAR | FIBRE | SALT |

£0.87 /PERSON · SERVES 4 · EASE ★★☆☆☆ · PREP 20 MINS · GF

SRI LANKAN FRIED RICE

Often, when we test recipes we have to go through numerous versions before we get it right. We don't know what happened with this one, but we managed to nail it first time! Well done us!

4 **eggs**

1 mug (250g) **basmati rice**

1 teaspoon **turmeric**

50g **butter**, measure using packet

1 **red onion**, chopped

4 **carrots**, peeled and diced

2 cloves **garlic**, chopped

1 **fat red chilli**, chopped

½ mug (100g) **cashew nuts**

2 mugs (300g) **frozen peas**, defrosted

2 tablespoons freshly chopped **coriander**

1 Put the eggs in a pan of boiling water and simmer for 10 minutes. Drain and run under a cold tap, carefully peel off the shells and roughly chop.

2 Put the rice in a saucepan with 2 mugs of boiling water and the turmeric. Bring to the boil and simmer gently, with a lid on the pan, for 10 minutes.

3 Heat the butter in a large frying pan or wok. Add the onions and carrots and fry for 5 minutes.

4 Add the garlic, chilli and cashews and fry for 1 minute.

5 Add the cooked rice to the pan, along with the peas. Season well with salt and pepper and fry for 2–3 minutes.

6 Serve with the eggs and coriander.

RDA 100%

| 520kcal CALORIES | 23g PROTEIN | 29g FAT | 11g SAT FAT | 51g CARBS | 11g SUGAR | 9g FIBRE | 0.6g SALT |

SMOKED PAPRIKA TOFU SALAD

Take your time when frying the tofu so you get a good even crust on all sides. Trust us, it will make all the difference.

1 tablespoon **smoked paprika**

250g **firm tofu**, cut into chunks

2 tablespoons **olive oil**

200g **baby leaf salad**

400g tin **black beans**, drained and rinsed

200g **ready-roasted red peppers** (from a jar), chopped

1 **avocado**, peeled and cut into small chunks

1 **red onion**, thinly sliced

DRESSING

juice of a **lime**

2 tablespoons **extra virgin olive oil**

1 tablespoon **maple syrup**

salt and **pepper**

1 Put the paprika on a large plate and add the tofu. Gently toss together to fully coat the tofu.

2 Heat the oil in a frying pan and gently fry the tofu until it browns on all sides.

3 Put the salad leaves in a large bowl, add the beans, peppers, avocado and onion.

4 Mix the dressing ingredients and add to the bowl, together with the cooked tofu. Gently mix together.

RDA 100%

361kcal	15g	24g	4g	21g	7g	8g	1g
CALORIES	PROTEIN	FAT	SAT FAT	CARBS	SUGAR	FIBRE	SALT

£ 1.91 /PERSON · SERVES 4 · EASE ★☆☆☆☆ · PREP 20 MINS · GF OPTION

DOLCELATTE AND AVOCADO SALAD

The balance of the avocado and blue cheese is what makes this a 'stand-out' salad.

GLUTEN-FREE OPTION: use GF bread.

1 **ciabatta**, cut into chunks

2 tablespoons **olive oil**

SALAD

3 **avocados**, peeled and cut into small chunks

2 tablespoons freshly chopped **chives**

1 bunch **spring onions**, sliced lengthways

bag **salad leaves**

200g **Dolcelatte**, crumbled

DRESSING

5 tablespoons **Greek yogurt**

juice of a **lemon**

2 tablespoons **extra virgin olive oil**

1 tablespoon **maple syrup**

salt and **pepper**

1　Heat the oil in a frying pan and add the ciabatta. Fry until browned on all sides.

2　Divide the salad ingredients between the four plates.

3　Mix the dressing ingredients and drizzle over each plate. Serve with the ciabatta.

RDA 100%

| 765kcal | 22g | 51g | 18g | 52g | 8g | 7g | 2g |
| CALORIES | PROTEIN | FAT | SAT FAT | CARBS | SUGAR | FIBRE | SALT |

QUINOA AND BEETROOT SALAD

Quinoa may seem like a new 'fad' ingredient, but it is full of protein and other good nutrition. Don't be tempted to use cooked beetroot.

½ mug (100g) **quinoa**

3 **raw beetroot**, peeled and thinly sliced or grated

200g **beansprouts**

⅓ mug (50g) **cranberries**

3 tablespoons (25g) **pumpkin seeds**

½ mug (50g) **flaked almonds**

DRESSING

3 tablespoons **cider vinegar**

3 tablespoons **extra virgin olive oil**

2 tablespoons **honey**

salt and **pepper**

bag **lamb's lettuce**

2 tablespoons **rapeseed oil**

4 **eggs**

1 Put the quinoa in a small saucepan of boiling, salted water. Simmer for 10 minutes. Drain and leave to cool slightly.

2 Put the beetroot, beansprouts, cranberries, pumpkin seed and almonds in a bowl. Mix together. Add the cooked quinoa.

3 Mix together the dressing ingredients and add to the salad.

4 Divide the salad between the plates, along with the lamb's lettuce.

5 Heat the oil in a large frying and fry the eggs. Allow them to frizzle a bit around the edges.

RDA 100%

527kcal	18g	38g	5g	27g	19g	5g	0.5g
CALORIES	PROTEIN	FAT	SAT FAT	CARBS	SUGAR	FIBRE	SALT

£1.04 /PERSON · SERVES 4 · EASE ★★☆☆☆ · PREP 25 MINS · GF

FETA ROSTI WITH PICKLED BEETROOT

If you are making lots of these, you can use a food processor to do the grating for you. It should save time and your fingertips! Don't be tempted to use cooked beetroot.

2 **raw beetroot**, peeled and cut into thin strips

2 tablespoons **cider vinegar**

1 tablespoon **maple syrup**

3 medium **potatoes,** grated

4 **spring onions,** finely sliced

200g **feta,** crumbled

2 tablespoons **olive oil**

SAUCE

4 tablespoons **crème fraîche**

juice of a **lemon**

2 tablespoons freshly chopped **basil**

salt and **pepper**

bag **lamb's lettuce**

1 Mix the beetroot with the vinegar and syrup and leave to stand for at least 10 minutes.

2 Mix the potatoes, spring onions and feta in a large bowl. Season well with salt and pepper. Divide the mixture into 4 and form into patties.

3 Heat the oil in a frying pan and fry the mixture on a medium heat, until browned on both sides.

4 Mix together the sauce ingredients and serve with everything else.

RDA 100%

395kcal	13g	22g	12g	33g	8g	4g	2g
CALORIES	PROTEIN	FAT	SAT FAT	CARBS	SUGAR	FIBRE	SALT

SESAME ASPARAGUS AND CRISPY EGGS

The trick with this recipe is making sure you don't brown the breadcrumbs too much before the egg is fully cooked. Take your time! We always use organic rapeseed oil.

GLUTEN-FREE OPTION: use GF bread.

---

3 slices **bread**

1 bunch **spring onions**, chopped

2 tablespoons **rapeseed oil**

4 **eggs**

350g **asparagus**

2 tablespoons **toasted sesame oil**

DRESSING

2 tablespoons freshly chopped **chives**

juice of 2 **lemons**

3 tablespoons **maple syrup**

salt and **pepper**

2 tablespoons **sesame seeds**

1 Blitz the bread, spring onions and 1 tablespoon of rapeseed oil in a food processor, until you have breadcrumbs.

2 Heat the other tablespoon of rapeseed oil in a large frying pan and make 4 piles of the breadcrumb mix in the pan. Spread out slightly and make a small 'dent' in the middle of each pile. Break an egg into each 'dent'. Fry gently on a low heat until the egg is cooked and the breadcrumbs browned and crisp.

3 Snap the tough ends off the asparagus and discard. Heat the sesame oil in a large frying pan. Add the asparagus and fry for 3–4 minutes until they begin to brown. Add the dressing and fry for another minute. The dressing should thicken and go sticky. Mix in the sesame seeds and remove from the pan.

RDA 100%

377kcal	16g	25g	4g	21g	10g	4g	1g
CALORIES	PROTEIN	FAT	SAT FAT	CARBS	SUGAR	FIBRE	SALT

CHEDDAR MUFFINS & ROASTED TOMATO SOUP

GLUTEN-FREE OPTION: use GF flour, baking powder + 1 teaspoon of xanthan gum in the muffins. Use a GF stock cube.

SOUP

2 **red onions**, cut into wedges

8 **tomatoes**, halved

2 cloves **garlic**, peeled

2 tablespoons **olive oil**

1 mug (300ml) **water**

1 **veg stock cube**

2 tablespoons **sun-dried tomato purée**

1 tablespoon **honey**

1 tablespoon **cider vinegar**

CHEESE MUFFINS

350g **self-raising flour**

1 teaspoon **baking powder**

1 mug (75g) grated **Cheddar cheese**

¼ mug (50g) **pine nuts**

2 teaspoons **smoked paprika**

3 **eggs**

250ml **milk**

TOPPING

½ mug (40g) grated **Cheddar cheese**

¼ mug (25g) **roasted chopped hazelnuts**

1 Preheat the oven to 180°C fan/200°C/gas 6. Put 12 muffin cases in a muffin tin.

2 Put the onions, tomatoes and garlic on a roasting tray. Drizzle with the oil and season well with salt and pepper. Mix everything together. Roast in the oven for 45 minutes.

3 Meanwhile, make the muffins by mixing the dry ingredients in a large mixing bowl.

4 Mix together the eggs and milk and season with salt and pepper. Add to the bowl and mix well.

5 Spoon into the muffin cases. Sprinkle over the cheese and hazelnuts. Bake in the oven for 25 minutes.

6 Put the rest of the soup ingredients in a large saucepan. Add the roasted vegetables and blitz with a hand-held blender. Season well with salt and pepper.

7 Simmer for 2–3 minutes.

RDA 100%

754kcal	32g	38g	11g	82g	21g	7g	2g
CALORIES	PROTEIN	FAT	SAT FAT	CARBS	SUGAR	FIBRE	SALT

JACKFRUIT BURGERS WITH SIMPLE SLAW

You can serve these with burger buns, chips or wedges if you like, but they are great on their own for a light lunch.

GLUTEN-FREE OPTION: use GF bread.

BURGERS

400g tin **jackfruit**, drained and rinsed

400g tin **chickpeas**, drained and rinsed

1 **onion**, quartered

2 cloves **garlic**, roughly chopped

3 tablespoons freshly chopped **coriander**

1 teaspoon **cumin**

1 **fat red chilli**, roughly chopped

1 tablespoon **tomato purée**

2 slices **bread**

3 tablespoons **olive oil**

SLAW

1 bunch **spring onions**, finely chopped

3 sticks **celery**, finely chopped

2 **carrots**, grated

1 **Little Gem lettuce**, finely sliced

2 tablespoons **peanut butter** (see p218)

2 tablespoons **extra virgin olive oil**

juice of a **lemon**

1 tablespoon **maple syrup**

1 Soak the jackfruit in a bowl of water for 10 minutes. Drain, squeeze out, and roughly chop.

2 Put the jackfruit, chickpeas, onion, garlic, coriander, cumin, chilli, tomato purée and bread in a processor and blitz. Season well with salt and pepper.

3 Take the mixture out of the processor and mould into 8 burgers.

4 Heat the oil in a large frying pan. Fry the burgers until they are nicely browned on each side.

5 Mix together the slaw ingredients and serve with the burgers.

RDA 100%

477kcal	13g	24g	4g	47g	13g	13g	1g
CALORIES	PROTEIN	FAT	SAT FAT	CARBS	SUGAR	FIBRE	SALT

BEETROOT AND ORANGE SALAD

Fruit in salads, especially when combined with cheese, in always a winner. The pop of juice you get every now and then is delicous. Use raw honey if you can (see p7).

GLUTEN-FREE OPTION: serve with GF bread.

DRESSING

1 tablespoon **runny honey**

1 teaspoon **wholegrain mustard**

1 tablespoon **white wine vinegar**

2 tablespoons **extra virgin olive oil**

salt and **pepper**

SALAD

bag **watercress salad**

bag **mixed salad leaves**

6 **spring onions**, thinly sliced

2 **oranges**, peeled and sliced

8 **ready-cooked beetroot**, diced

150g **soft, vegetarian goat's cheese**

crusty bread

1 Mix together the dressing ingredients.

2 Mix together the watercress, salad leaves and onion.

3 Divide the salad ingredients between the plates, with the oranges and beetroot on top. Cut or tear the cheese into 'blobs' and scatter over the salad.

4 Drizzle the dressing over and serve with crusty bread.

RDA 100%

540kcal	21g	20g	9g	69g	22g	8g	2g
CALORIES	PROTEIN	FAT	SAT FAT	CARBS	SUGAR	FIBRE	SALT

£ 1.70 /PERSON — SERVES 4 — EASE ★★☆☆☆ — PREP 20 MINS — GF OPTION

SLICED TORTILLA AND AVOCADO SALAD

Strips of crunchy, fried tortilla add a great texture to this salad.

GLUTEN-FREE OPTION: use GF wraps.

2 tablespoons **toasted sesame oil**

4 **tortilla wraps**, cut into strips

2 **avocados**, peeled and cut into small chunks

1 **Romaine lettuce**, sliced

1/2 **cucumber**, cut into chunks

1 **fat red chilli**, chopped

200g **cherry tomatoes**, halved

200g **feta cheese**, crumbled

DRESSING

2 tablespoons **extra virgin olive oil**

juice of 1 **lemon**

1/2 mug (150ml) **Greek yogurt**

2/3 mug (100g) **pistachios**, chopped

salt and **pepper**

1 Heat the oil in a frying pan, add the wrap strips and fry until golden brown. Remove from the pan.

2 Put the avocados, lettuce, cucumber, chilli and tomatoes in a bowl and mix. Divide between the plates.

3 Top with the feta and strips of tortilla on top.

4 Mix the dressing ingredients together and drizzle over the salad.

RDA 100%

| 756kcal | 23g | 54g | 17g | 44g | 9g | 14g | 4g |
| CALORIES | PROTEIN | FAT | SAT FAT | CARBS | SUGAR | FIBRE | SALT |

   GF Ve

PINK GRAPEFRUIT SALAD AND WEDGES

Pink grapefruit in a salad might seem to be an aquired taste to some, but you just have to try it once to be a believer! Browning the tofu is essential here.

4 medium **potatoes**, cut into wedges

2 tablespoons **olive oil**

2 **pink grapefruits**

1 bunch **spring onions**, chopped

½ mug (50g) roughly chopped **pecans**

DRESSING

2 tablespoons **extra virgin olive oil**

2 tablespoons **cider vinegar**

1 tablespoon **maple syrup**

salt and **pepper**

280g **firm tofu**, cut into chunks

1 tablespoon **toasted sesame oil**

bag **watercress**

2 **ripe avocados**, peeled and sliced

1 Preheat the oven to 180°C fan/200°C/gas 6.

2 Put the potato wedges on a large roasting tray and drizzle with the oil. Season well with salt and pepper. Mix everything together and then spread out evenly. Roast in the oven for 40–50 minutes, or until nicely browned.

3 Peel the grapefruits with a knife, removing all the pith. Cut the segments out of the grapefruits and place in a large bowl, along with the spring onions and pecans.

4 Mix the dressing ingredients and add to the bowl.

5 Heat the sesame oil in a frying pan and fry the tofu until it is browned on as many sides as possible.

6 Add the watercress to the salad and divide between the plates. Serve the tofu and avocado on top and the wedges to one side.

RDA 100%

669kcal	17g	41g	6g	52g	19g	10g	1g
CALORIES	PROTEIN	FAT	SAT FAT	CARBS	SUGAR	FIBRE	SALT

£ 1.66 /PERSON · SERVES 4 · EASE ★★☆☆☆ · PREP 20 MINS · GF Ve

BLACK BEAN RICE WITH SWEET CHILLI SAUCE

The combination of flavours and textures makes this dish a winner.

1 mug (250g) **basmati rice**

½ teaspoon **turmeric**

1 teaspoon **cumin**

1 teaspoon **ground coriander**

400g tin **black beans**, drained and rinsed

200g tin **sweetcorn**, drained

200g **cherry tomatoes**, halved

1 **red onion**, thinly sliced

ruby gem lettuce, sliced

2 tablespoons freshly chopped **coriander**

2 **avocados**

juice of a **lime**

sweet chilli sauce (see p219)

1 Put the rice, turmeric, cumin and coriander in a saucepan, with 2 mugs of boiling water. Bring to the boil and simmer gently, with a lid on the pan, for 10 minutes.

2 Tip out onto a plate to cool.

3 Put the beans, sweetcorn, tomatoes, onion, lettuce and fresh coriander in a large bowl. Add the cooled rice and stir.

4 Peel the avocados and cut into cubes. Toss in the lime juice. Add to the salad, season well with salt and pepper, and mix.

5 Serve with some sweet chilli sauce over the top of each serving.

RDA 100%

313kcal	11g	12g	3g	52g	9g	10g	0.2g
CALORIES	PROTEIN	FAT	SAT FAT	CARBS	SUGAR	FIBRE	SALT

£2.12 /PERSON · SERVES 4 · EASE ★★☆☆ · PREP 25 MINS · COOK 50 MINS · GF OPTION

CASHEW NUT BURGERS

The mix of textures in the slaw, coming from the crunchy cabbage, the juicy apple and the popping pumpkin seeds, makes a great accompaniment to the burgers.

GLUTEN-FREE OPTION: use GF bread.

4 **sweet potatoes**, cut into wedges
2 tablespoons **olive oil**

BURGERS

2 mugs (400g) **cashew nuts**
1 **onion**, chopped
2 slices **bread**
2 cloves **garlic**, chopped
250g **chestnut mushrooms**
2 tablespoons freshly chopped **coriander**
1 **egg**, beaten
1 tablespoon **olive oil**

RED CABBAGE AND APPLE SLAW

1 **Granny Smith**, thinly sliced
½ **red cabbage**, thinly sliced
2 tablespoons **pumpkin seeds**
½ mug (100g) **raisins**
2 tablespoons **olive oil**
1 tablespoon **cider vinegar**
1 tablespoon **honey**

1 Preheat the oven to 180°C fan/200°C/gas 6.

2 Put the sweet potatoes on a roasting tray, drizzle with the oil, and season with salt and pepper. Roast in the oven for 50 minutes.

3 Put the nuts, onion, bread and garlic in a food processor and blitz until things look like breadcrumbs. Tip out into a large mixing bowl.

4 Put the mushrooms and coriander in the processor and blitz until it also looks like breadcrumbs. Add to the bowl. Season well with salt and pepper.

5 Beat the egg and add to the bowl. Mix together and then form into 8 burgers. Set to one side.

6 When the potatoes have 10 minutes left to cook, heat the oil in a frying pan and fry the burgers on each side, on a medium heat, until nicely browned.

7 Meanwhile, mix together the slaw ingredients.

58

RDA 100%

1179kcal	31g	71g	13g	108g	32g	15g	1g
CALORIES	PROTEIN	FAT	SAT FAT	CARBS	SUGAR	FIBRE	SALT

ROAST SQUASH SALAD

I am starting to think we might be addicted to adding fruit to salads. Either way, here we go again, this time with some lovely sweet and sharp cranberries to go with the feta.

1 **butternut squash**, peeled and sliced

2 **red onions**, cut into wedges

2 tablespoons **olive oil**

2 tablespoons **harissa paste**

250g **ready-to-eat puy lentils**

DRESSING

2 tablespoons **extra virgin olive oil**

2 tablespoons **cider vinegar**

1 tablespoon **honey**

salt and **pepper**

bag **rocket salad**

½ mug (70g) **cranberries**

200g **feta cheese**, crumbled

1 Preheat the oven to 180°C fan/200°C/gas 6.

2 Put the squash and onions on a large roasting tray. Drizzle with the oil and harissa paste. Season with salt and pepper and mix everything together. Spread out and roast in the oven for 40 minutes.

3 Add the lentils to the roasting tray and roast for a further 10 minutes.

4 Mix together the dressing, rocket and cranberries. Divide between the plates.

5 Serve everything together with the feta on top.

RDA 100%

506kcal	16g	28g	11g	42g	24g	11g	1g
CALORIES	PROTEIN	FAT	SAT FAT	CARBS	SUGAR	FIBRE	SALT

FRIED PEAR AND DOLCELATTE SALAD

Warm and delicately sweet pears and blue cheese. What a combo!

GLUTEN-FREE OPTION: use GF bread.

---

2 tablespoons **olive oil**

4 slices **seeded bread**

50g **butter**, measure using packet

2 tablespoons **coconut sugar**

3 **conference pears**, peeled and cut into 8

juice of a **lemon**

bag **rocket salad**

½ **cucumber**, sliced

4 **spring onions**, finely sliced, lengthways

2 tablespoons freshly chopped **coriander**

200g **dolcelatte cheese**, crumbled

1 Heat the oil in a frying pan and add the bread. Fry until browned on both sides. Remove from the pan and cut into croutons.

2 Put the butter and sugar into a frying pan and gently heat. Add the pears and cook for 2–3 minutes. Remove the pears from the pan and add the lemon juice to make the dressing.

3 Mix together the rocket, cucumber, onions, coriander and croutons. Divide between the plates.

4 Serve the pears on top of the salad, with the cheese and dressing poured over.

RDA 100%

| 513kcal | 15g | 36g | 19g | 31g | 12g | 4g | 2g |
| CALORIES | PROTEIN | FAT | SAT FAT | CARBS | SUGAR | FIBRE | SALT |

KALE BURGER

If you are still on the fence with the whole 'kale' thing, give this burger a try, you are sure to be won over.

GLUTEN-FREE OPTION: use GF buns.

3 tablespoons **olive oil**

1 **onion**, roughly chopped

2 cloves **garlic**, sliced

100g **kale**, chopped

250g **ready-cooked quinoa**

2 slices **bread**

6 **sun-dried tomatoes**

1 **egg yolk**

1 **red onion**, sliced

25g **butter**, measure using packet

1 tablespoon **olive oil**

4 **brioche burger buns**

100g **cottage cheese**

bag **rocket salad leaves**

1 Heat 1 tablespoon of the oil in a large frying pan and add the chopped onions and garlic. Fry until the onions begin to brown lightly. Transfer to a food processor.

2 Put the kale in the frying pan with ½ mug of water. Bring to the boil and then simmer, with a lid on the pan, for 2 minutes. Remove the lid and boil off any excess water.

3 Transfer to a food processor. Season well with salt and pepper and add the quinoa, bread and tomatoes. Blitz and then add the egg yolk. Pulse a couple of times. Form the mixture into 4 burgers.

4 Put the 2 tablespoons of oil in the frying pan and fry the burgers, on a gentle heat, until lightly browned on both sides.

5 Put the sliced red onions, butter and oil in a small frying pan and fry the onions, on a medium heat, until caramelised. This may take 5–10 minutes.

6 Toast the burger buns. Construct the burgers by adding the burger, then a dollop of cottage cheese and then the onions. Serve with the rocket.

RDA 100%

660kcal	20g	32g	9g	68g	15g	10g	2g
CALORIES	PROTEIN	FAT	SAT FAT	CARBS	SUGAR	FIBRE	SALT

£ 1.31 /PERSON   SERVES 4   EASE ★☆☆☆☆   COOK 15 MINS   GF OPTION

HONEYDEW MELON AND FETA SALAD

Mixing a bit of heat from the chillies with honeydew melon salad - you have to try it!

GLUTEN-FREE OPTION: use GF pitta bread.

---

1 **honeydew melon**, peeled, deseeded and chopped

2 tablespoons freshly chopped **coriander**

2 tablespoons freshly chopped **mint**

2 tablespoons **pumpkin seeds**

200g **cherry tomatoes**, halved

1 bunch **spring onions**, chopped

DRESSING

½ **fat red chilli**, chopped

2 tablespoons **extra virgin olive oil**

juice of a **lime**

1 tablespoon **maple syrup**

salt and **pepper**

200g **feta**

4 **pitta breads**

1 Place the melon in a large bowl and add the rest of the salad ingredients.

2 Mix the dressing ingredients together and add to the bowl. Divide between the plates and crumble over the feta.

3 Warm the pitta breads and serve with the salad.

RDA 100%

| 547kcal CALORIES | 19g PROTEIN | 25g FAT | 11g SAT FAT | 64g CARBS | 33g SUGAR | 8g FIBRE | 2g SALT |

JACKFRUIT SLOPPY JOES

Ridiculously moreish, and fantastically messy to eat. Promise us you won't wimp out and eat this with a knife and fork - it just won't be the same.

GLUTEN-FREE OPTION: use GF bread and stock cubes.

1 tablespoon **olive oil**

2 **onions**, sliced

1 tablespoon **olive oil**

1 **onion**, chopped

2 cloves **garlic**, chopped

400g tin **jackfruit**, drained, rinsed and roughly chopped

1 tablespoon **pomegranate molasses**

2 teaspoons **smoked paprika**

½ mug (150ml) **water**

1 **veg stock cube**

½ **pointy sweetheart cabbage**, thinly sliced

3 **carrots**, peeled and grated

3 tablespoons **maple syrup**

2 **ciabatta loaves**, halved

1 Heat the oil in a frying pan and add the two onions. Season well with salt and pepper and fry on a medium heat for about 10 minutes, stirring frequently. The onions should turn a lovely brown colour.

2 Meanwhile, heat the other tablespoon of olive oil in another frying pan or wok. Add the other onion and garlic and fry for 2 minutes.

3 Add the jackfruit and fry for 4 minutes, or until the jackfruit begins to soften.

4 Add the pomegranate molasses, paprika, water and stock and bring to the boil. Simmer for 2–3 minutes until the sauce thickens.

5 Mix the cabbage, carrots and maple syrup together to make a simple slaw.

6 Serve the slaw on the ciabatta, add the jackfruit mix and top with the caramelised onions.

RDA 100%

823kcal	24g	17g	3g	136g	31g	17g	2g
CALORIES	PROTEIN	FAT	SAT FAT	CARBS	SUGAR	FIBRE	SALT

£ 1.47 /PERSON · SERVES 4 · EASE ★★☆☆☆ · PREP 15 MINS · GF OPTION

CHICORY AND EGG SALAD

Lovely fresh salad. The bitterness of the chicory is offset by the sweet dressing.

GLUTEN-FREE OPTION: use GF bread.

8 **eggs**
2 tablespoons **olive oil**
3 slices **bread**
bag **salad leaves**
2 **chicory**, sliced
1 bunch **spring onions**, sliced

DRESSING

1 teaspoon **Dijon mustard**
2 tablespoons **white wine vinegar**
2 tablespoons **extra virgin olive oil**
1 tablespoon **maple syrup**
salt and **pepper**

200g **feta**
coconut crisps (see p216)

1 Put the eggs in a pan of boiling water and simmer for 5 minutes. Drain and run the eggs under the cold water. Carefully peel.

2 Meanwhile, put the oil in a large frying pan and fry the slices of bread. Take out of the pan and cut into croutons.

3 Put the salad leaves, chicory and spring onions in a large bowl. Add the croutons.

4 Mix the dressing ingredients together and add to the salad bowl.

5 Divide the salad amongst the plates. Crumble over the feta.

6 Add the eggs and coconut crisps.

RDA 100%

549kcal CALORIES | 31g PROTEIN | 40g FAT | 15g SAT FAT | 17g CARBS | 6g SUGAR | 4g FIBRE | 2g SALT

£ 1.87 /PERSON · SERVES 4 · EASE ★★☆☆☆ · PREP 20 MINS · GF Ve OPTION

SESAME SEED TOFU WITH BEANSPROUT SALAD

Tofu in itself can be quite bland, but mixing with the spices and seeds and frying transforms it.

VEGAN OPTION: use maple syrup instead of honey.

2 x 280g packets **firm tofu**

4 tablespoons **sesame seeds**

2 tablespoons **black sesame seeds**

2 tablespoons **cornflour**

1 tablespoon **ground ginger**

2 tablespoons **smoked paprika**

BEANSPROUT SALAD

100g **beansprouts**

½ **cucumber**, sliced

1 **red onion**, thinly sliced

1 **Little Gem lettuce**

DRESSING

2 tablespoons **extra virgin olive oil**

1 tablespoon **pomegranate molasses**

juice of a **lime**

1 tablespoon **honey**

salt and **pepper**

2 tablespoons **rapeseed oil**

1 Slice each piece of tofu lengthways into 8 slices. In a bowl, mix together the seeds, cornflour, ginger and paprika. Season with salt and pepper. Dip the tofu in the mixture and rub in.

2 Mix the salad ingredients in a large bowl.

3 Combine the dressing ingredients and add to the bowl.

4 Heat the oil in a large frying pan and fry the tofu slices. You may need to fry in 2 batches.

5 Serve the tofu with the salad.

RDA 100%

475kcal	24g	35g	5g	13g	10g	5g	2
CALORIES	PROTEIN	FAT	SAT FAT	CARBS	SUGAR	FIBRE	SALT

MOROCCAN CARROT SALAD WITH GOAT'S CHEESE

Crunchy coated, melted cheese. My mouth is watering just looking at it.

GLUTEN-FREE OPTION: use GF bread.

SALAD

5 **carrots**, grated

zest and juice of an **orange**

2 tablespoons **maple syrup**

20 **green olives**, roughly chopped

2 **preserved lemons**, chopped

4 tablespoons freshly chopped **coriander**

2 tablespoons **extra virgin olive oil**

1 **red onion**, chopped

½ mug (100g) **cashew nuts**

300g **vegetarian goat's cheese**

1 **egg**, beaten

2 slices **bread**, made into breadcrumbs

2 tablespoons **olive oil**

1 Mix together the salad ingredients. Season well with salt and pepper.

2 Cut the cheese into 1cm slices. Dip them in the beaten egg and then into the breadcrumbs.

3 Heat the oil in a large frying pan and fry the cheese, on a medium heat, until lightly browned on both sides.

4 Serve with the salad.

RDA 100%

699kcal	26g	52g	20g	29g	17g	7g	3g
CALORIES	PROTEIN	FAT	SAT FAT	CARBS	SUGAR	FIBRE	SALT

ROAST PARSNIP AND HALLOUMI SALAD

We love recipes like this, where, essentially, you just shove everything in the oven at different times. What you are left with is a selection of roasted goodness.

4 medium **parsnips**, peeled and cut into chunks

2 **red onions**, cut into wedges

250g **mushrooms**, halved

2 tablespoons **olive oil**

400g tin **cannellini beans**, drained and rinsed

²/₃ mug (100g) **macadamia nuts**

250g **halloumi**, cut into chunks

200g **spinach**, roughly chopped

DRESSING

¼ mug (75ml) **apple juice**

2 tablespoons **extra virgin olive oil**

2 tablespoons **balsamic vinegar**

salt and **pepper**

1 Preheat the oven to 180°C fan/200°C/gas 6.

2 Put the parsnips, onions and mushrooms on a large roasting tray. Drizzle with the oil, season well with salt and pepper, mix together and spread out on the tray. Roast in the oven for 25 minutes.

3 After 25 minutes, put the beans, nuts and halloumi on another tray. Drizzle with oil and season well. Mix everything together and then spread out. Roast everything in the oven for a further 25 minutes.

4 Meanwhile, mix the dressing ingredients together.

5 When the veggies and beans, etc. are cooked, take out of the oven. Transfer to a mixing bowl along with the spinach. Gently mix together.

6 Drizzle over the dressing.

RDA 100%

| 643kcal | 26g | 44g | 16g | 30g | 14g | 12g | 2g |
| CALORIES | PROTEIN | FAT | SAT FAT | CARBS | SUGAR | FIBRE | SALT |

CHESTNUT EN CROÛTE

Delicious, blue cheese and chestnuts wrapped in gorgeous, flaky pastry.

GLUTEN-FREE OPTION: use GF bread and pastry.

1 **onion**, chopped

200g **whole, cooked chestnuts**

1 slice **bread**

1 **egg yolk**

75g **spinach**, roughly chopped

400g tin **cannellini beans**, drained and rinsed

200g **blue Stilton**

280g pack **ready-rolled puff pastry**

beaten **egg**, to glaze

SALAD

1 bag **salad leaves**

1 **apple**, thinly sliced

4 **spring onions**, sliced

DRESSING

juice of a **lemon**

1 tablespoon **honey**

2 tablespoons **extra virgin olive oil**

salt and **pepper**

beetroot pickle (see p215)

1 Preheat the oven to 200°C fan/220°C/gas 7.

2 Prepare a large roasting tray, with a silicone sheet, or greaseproof paper.

3 Put the onion, chestnuts and bread in the food processor and blitz until you have something resembling breadcrumbs. Alternatively, just chop finely.

4 Add the egg yolk, spinach, beans and cheese. Season well with salt and pepper and pulse a couple of times.

5 Lay the pastry sheet on the roasting tray. Pile the filling down the middle and squish into a long sausage shape. Brush the edges of the pastry with a little water. Fold over and pinch together, creating a sealed 'parcel'.

6 Brush the top with beaten egg and bake in the oven for 30 minutes.

7 Mix together the salad ingredients. Add the dressing. Serve with the beetroot pickle.

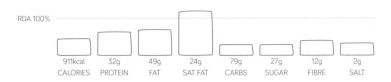

RDA 100%

911kcal	32g	49g	24g	79g	27g	12g	2g
CALORIES	PROTEIN	FAT	SAT FAT	CARBS	SUGAR	FIBRE	SALT

£1.38 /PERSON · SERVES 4 · EASE ★★☆☆☆ · PREP 15 MINS · Ve GF OPTION

PEANUT AND SOY BEAN NOODLES

GLUTEN-FREE OPTION: use GF soy sauce.

200g **ribbon rice noodles**

1 mug (200g) **peanuts**

2 tablespoons **toasted sesame oil**

1 clove **garlic**, chopped

1 **red pepper**, chopped

1 tablespoon freshly grated **ginger**

1 bunch **spring onions**, chopped

1 mug (150g) **frozen soy beans**, defrosted

SAUCE

400ml tin **coconut milk**

1 **fat red chilli**, chopped

2 tablespoons **soy sauce**

2 tablespoons **peanut butter** (see p218)

2 tablespoons **water**

1 tablespoon **cider vinegar**

1 Put the noodles in a large bowl and cover with boiling water. Leave to stand for 10 minutes. Drain and return to the bowl.

2 Meanwhile, heat the wok or large frying pan, add the peanuts and dry-fry until they begin to brown lightly.

3 Add the oil, garlic, pepper, ginger and spring onions and fry for 2 minutes.

4 Add the soy beans and fry for 1 minute.

5 Mix together the sauce ingredients and add to the pan. Simmer for 2 minutes.

6 Serve with the rice noodles.

RDA 100%

832kcal CALORIES	30g PROTEIN	53g FAT	18g SAT FAT	54g CARBS	9g SUGAR	10g FIBRE	2g SALT

BEETROOT TIMBALES

GLUTEN-FREE OPTION: use GF flour.

500g **raw beetroot**, peeled and cut into chunks

1 mug (300ml) **water**

4 tablespoons **cider vinegar**

1 tablespoon **coconut sugar**

2 **red onions**, cut into wedges

4 **sweet potatoes**, cut into chunks

4 **parsnips**, cut into chunks

3 **eggs**

2 tablespoons **double cream**

5 tablespoons **self-raising flour**

SAUCE

50g **butter**, measure using packet

1 tablespoon **plain flour**

1 mug (300ml) **milk**

2 tablespoons freshly chopped **chives**

1 Preheat the oven to 180°C fan/200°C/gas 6.

2 Put the beetroot, water, vinegar and coconut sugar in a small saucepan and bring to the boil. Simmer for 20 minutes with a lid on the pan. Drain and return to the pan. Leave to cool a little.

3 Put the onions, sweet potatoes and parsnips on a large roasting tray. Season with salt and pepper and drizzle with oil. Mix everything together and spread out. Roast in the oven for 50 minutes.

4 Meanwhile, put the eggs, cream and flour in a blender and blitz until smooth. Season well with salt and pepper. Add the cooled, drained beetroot and blend.

5 Grease 6 ramekin dishes and place on a roasting tin. Divide the blended mixture between them and bake in the oven for 35 minutes.

6 Meanwhile, make the sauce. Put the butter in a small saucepan and heat. Add the flour and mix together. Add the milk and bring the boil. Add the chives and simmer for 1 minute.

7 Serve with the timbales and the roasted veg.

RDA 100%

| 704kcal | 22g | 24g | 12g | 97g | 41g | 13g | 1g |
| CALORIES | PROTEIN | FAT | SAT FAT | CARBS | SUGAR | FIBRE | SALT |

AUBERGINE SCHNITZEL

It might seem a little over the top to arrange the potatoes in the casserole dish as we have done here (and maybe it is). The point isn't to make it look fancy, rather, to make sure all the potatoes cook and brown evenly.

GLUTEN-FREE OPTION: use GF bread.

5 medium **potatoes**, thinly sliced

2 tablespoons **olive oil**

2 **aubergines**, sliced into 4, lengthways

2 **eggs**

4 slices **bread**

20g **butter**, measure using packet

2 **spring onions**, chopped

1 stick **celery**, chopped

2 tablespoons **horseradish sauce**

12 **cherry tomatoes**, chopped

1 Preheat the oven to 180°C fan/200°C/gas 6.

2 Arrange the potatoes in layers in a casserole dish. Add the oil and season well with salt and pepper. Bake in the oven for 55 minutes.

3 Sprinkle salt over the aubergine slices and leave to rest for 30 minutes. Blot dry with kitchen towel.

4 Beat the eggs in a bowl.

5 Put the bread in a food processor and blitz until you have breadcrumbs. Pour out on a plate and season well with salt and pepper.

6 Dip the aubergine slices, first in the egg, and then in the breadcrumbs. Place on a roasting tray and roast in the oven for 15 minutes.

7 Meanwhile, make the sauce. Put the butter in a small frying pan and fry the onions and celery until they are soft. Add the horseradish and mix.

8 Serve with the tomatoes on the side.

RDA 100%

457kcal	14g	17g	5g	60g	8g	9g	1g
CALORIES	PROTEIN	FAT	SAT FAT	CARBS	SUGAR	FIBRE	SALT

WILD RICE WITH SPINACH AND CASHEWS

Nutty wild rice, nutty cashew nuts. I'm really surprised that the word 'nutty' doesn't actually feature in the title of this recipe. Maybe next re-print!

GLUTEN-FREE OPTION: use GF stock cubes.

³/₄ mug (190g) **mixed wild rice**

2 tablespoons **olive oil**

1 **red onion**, chopped

2 **carrots**, grated

2 cloves **garlic**, finely chopped

125g **mushrooms**, sliced

¹/₂ mug (150ml) **water**

1 **veg stock cube**

2 tablespoons **tomato purée**

1 teaspoon **cumin**

1 teaspoon **ground coriander**

200g **spinach**, roughly chopped

¹/₂ mug (100g) **cashew nuts**

1 Put the rice in a saucepan with 2 mugs of boiling water. Bring to the boil and simmer gently, with a lid on the pan, for 25 minutes.

2 10 minutes before the rice is cooked, heat the oil in a wok, or large frying pan. Add the onion, carrots and garlic. Fry until things begin to brown.

3 Add the mushrooms, water, stock cube, tomato purée, cumin and coriander. Season well with salt and pepper. Bring to the boil and then simmer for 5 minutes.

4 Add the cooked rice to the pan, along with the spinach and cashews. The spinach will wilt.

RDA 100%

443kcal	13g	20g	4g	50g	8g	5g	0.5g
CALORIES	PROTEIN	FAT	SAT FAT	CARBS	SUGAR	FIBRE	SALT

CRISPY POLENTA WITH ROAST VEG

You can buy pre-made polenta, which is totally fine. We use it sometimes, but, if you make it yourself, you can put flavour into it. Here, we have used vegetable stock.

GLUTEN-FREE OPTION: use GF stock cubes.

4 mugs (1200ml) boiling **water**

1 mug (200g) **fine polenta**

3 **veg stock cubes**

2 **red onions**, cut into wedges

3 **courgettes**, cut into chunks

2 tablespoons **rapeseed oil**

400g **cherry tomatoes**

250ml **Greek yogurt**

zest of a **lemon**

2 tablespoons freshly chopped **chives**

1 Put the boiling water in a large saucepan and add the polenta and stock cubes. Simmer and stir frequently for 10 minutes. The polenta will thicken. Take the pan off the heat.

2 Grease a 35 x 25cm roasting tray. Pour in the polenta mix and spread it out. It should be about 1cm thick. Leave to set for about 2 hours. Once set, remove from the tray and cut into triangles.

3 Preheat the oven to 200°C fan/220°C/gas 7. Put the polenta triangles on a roasting tray and carefully coat both sides with oil. Roast in the oven for 50 minutes, or until nicely browned.

4 On another tray, add the onions and courgettes, along with the oil, and carefully mix. Season well with salt and pepper. Roast in the oven for 30 minutes. Add the tomatoes and roast for a further 15 minutes.

5 Mix together the yogurt, lemon and chives.

6 Serve the polenta triangles with the roast veg, together with a blob of the sauce.

RDA 100%

400kcal	6g	15g	5g	54g	13g	5g	0.1g
CALORIES	PROTEIN	FAT	SAT FAT	CARBS	SUGAR	FIBRE	SALT

ROAST BEETROOT WITH STILTON RISOTTO

This is basically an amazing Stilton risotto, made extra amazing with roasted, red onions and crunchy chickpeas.

GLUTEN-FREE OPTION: use GF stock cubes.

3 **raw beetroots**, peeled and cut into wedges

2 **red onions**, cut into wedges

1 tablespoon **olive oil**

400g tin **chickpeas**, drained and rinsed

juice of ½ **lemon**

1 tablespoon **olive oil**

1 bunch **spring onions**, chopped

2 cloves **garlic**, chopped

1 mug (215g) **arborio rice**

1 **veg stock cube**

220g **Stilton cheese**, crumbled

1 Preheat the oven to 180°C fan/200°C/gas 6.

2 Place the beetroots and onions on a roasting tray and drizzle with olive oil. Season well with salt and pepper and mix everything together. Spread out and roast in the oven for 30 minutes.

3 Add the chickpeas to the tray and roast for 10 minutes. Remove from the oven and add the lemon juice.

4 Meanwhile, make the risotto. Heat the oil in a large frying pan and add the spring onions and garlic. Fry for 1 minute.

5 Add the rice and allow it to absorb the oil.

6 Add 2 mugs of water and the stock cube. Bring to the boil and simmer, with a lid on the pan, for 10 minutes. Add a little water if the risotto has gone too dry.

7 Add the cheese and stir in.

RDA 100%

620kcal	25g	30g	14g	61g	11g	7g	2g
CALORIES	PROTEIN	FAT	SAT FAT	CARBS	SUGAR	FIBRE	SALT

CURRIED NUT AND LENTIL ROAST

Nut roasts are one of those things that you don't often think to cook, but every time you do cook one, you think, "I love nut roasts, why don't I make them more often?".

GLUTEN-FREE OPTION: use GF bread.

LENTIL ROAST

1 tablespoon **rapeseed oil**

1 tablespoon **cumin seeds**

2 **onions**, finely chopped

2 cloves **garlic**, finely chopped

4 tablespoons **korma curry paste**

250g **chestnut mushrooms**, sliced

200g **paneer cheese**, grated

2 medium **carrots**, grated

400g tin **green lentils**, drained and rinsed

2 **tomatoes**, chopped

1 mug (200g) **cashew nuts**, chopped

2 tablespoons freshly chopped **coriander**

2 slices **bread**, made into breadcrumbs

4 **eggs**

1 tablespoon **olive oil**

1 **pointy sweetheart cabbage**, sliced

2 tablespoons **cider vinegar**

1 tablespoon **honey**

½ mug (150ml) **water**

salt and **pepper**

1 Preheat the oven to 170°C fan/ 190°C/gas 5. Grease a casserole dish.

2 Heat the oil in a frying pan. Add the cumin seeds, onions and garlic and fry for 2 minutes.

3 Add the korma paste and mix. Turn out into a large bowl.

4 Add the rest of the lentil roast ingredients and mix. Pour into the casserole dish and press down.

5 Bake in the oven for 35 minutes.

6 Heat the oil in a wok, or large saucepan. Add the cabbage and fry for 3 minutes, or until it begins to brown a little. Add the rest of the ingredients and simmer for 5 minutes, with a lid on the pan.

94

RDA 100%

874kcal	40g	51g	14g	55g	29g	15g	2g
CALORIES	PROTEIN	FAT	SAT FAT	CARBS	SUGAR	FIBRE	SALT

JACKFRUIT TACOS

Classic 'street food' with the texture of pulled pork. Jackfruit is grown in tropical areas and is a great source of protein, fibre and potassium.

GUACAMOLE

1 **fat red chilli**, chopped
2 **avocados**, peeled and mashed
juice of a **lime**
1 tablespoon **rapeseed oil**

SALSA

100g **cherry tomatoes**, chopped
1 **green chilli**, finely chopped
½ **red onion**, finely chopped
1 tablespoon **coconut sugar**
juice of ½ **lemon**

1 tablespoon **rapeseed oil**
1 **onion**, chopped
4 cloves **garlic**, chopped
2 x 400g tin **jackfruit**, drained and roughly chopped
1 **veg stock cube**
1 tablespoon **cornflour**
2 teaspoons **cumin**
2 teaspoons **smoked paprika**
2 tablespoons freshly chopped **coriander**
8 **taco shells**

1 Mix together the guacamole ingredients.

2 Mix the salsa ingredients together.

3 Heat the oil in a frying pan and add the onion and garlic. Fry until the onions soften. Add the jackfruit and fry for 2 minutes.

4 Mix together 1 mug (300ml) of water, the stock cube, cornflour, cumin and paprika, and add to the pan. Season well with salt and pepper and simmer for 2 minutes.

5 Add the coriander and take off the heat.

6 Fill the tacos with the guacamole, salsa and jackfruit.

RDA 100%

500kcal	8g	24g	3g	60g	9g	15g	1g
CALORIES	PROTEIN	FAT	SAT FAT	CARBS	SUGAR	FIBRE	SALT

SHIITAKE MUSHROOM LAKSA

A distinctively flavoured curry paste here and so easy to make. Give it a try.

CURRY PASTE

2 **lemon grass stalks**, outer layer removed

2 teaspoons **turmeric**

2 teaspoons **fennel seeds**

2 tablespoons peeled and roughly chopped **ginger**

1 **fat red chilli**

3 cloves **garlic**

½ mug (100g) **cashew nuts**

30g **fresh coriander**

juice of a **lime**

1 tablespoon **coconut sugar**

400ml tin **coconut milk**

1 ½ mugs (375g) **basmati rice**

2 tablespoons **rapeseed oil**

125g **shiitake mushrooms**

125g **chestnut mushrooms**, halved

350g **baby sweetcorn**, sliced lengthways

150g **mangetout**

2 tablespoons **black sesame seeds**, to garnish

1 Put the curry paste ingredients in a blender and blitz until smooth. No need to chop anything beforehand, just throw it in whole. Season with salt and pepper.

2 Put the rice in a saucepan with 3 mugs of boiling water. Bring to the boil and simmer gently, with a lid on the pan, for 10 minutes.

3 Heat the oil in a frying pan, or wok, add the mushrooms, sweetcorn and mangetout and fry for 2 minutes. Season well with salt and pepper.

4 Add the curry paste to the pan and bring to the boil. Simmer for 2 minutes.

5 Garnish with the sesame seeds.

RDA 100%

560kcal	19g	38g	16g	69g	12g	9g	0.2g
CALORIES	PROTEIN	FAT	SAT FAT	CARBS	SUGAR	FIBRE	SALT

   GF Ve

TOFU PAD THAI

GLUTEN-FREE OPTION: use GF soy sauce and stock cubes.

SAUCE

¾ mug (225ml) **water**

1 **veg stock cube**

3 tablespoons **mirin rice wine vinegar**

1 tablespoon **tamarind paste**

juice of a **lime**

3 tablespoons **coconut sugar**

2 tablespoons **soy sauce**

1 tablespoon **cornflour**

300g **rice noodles**

2 tablespoons **toasted sesame oil**

½ mug (100g) **unsalted peanuts**, roughly chopped

1 bunch **spring onions**, chopped

2 **pak choi**, sliced

280g **firm tofu**, cut into small chunks

2 tablespoons freshly chopped **coriander**

1 Mix together the sauce ingredients.

2 Put the rice noodles in a large bowl and cover with boiling water. Leave to stand for 10 minutes. Drain and return to the bowl.

3 Meanwhile, put the oil in a wok or frying pan. Add the peanuts and fry for 1 minute. Add the spring onions, pak choi and tofu pieces. Fry for 2–3 minutes.

4 Add the sauce ingredients and bring to the boil.

5 Mix with the noodles and garnish with the coriander.

RDA 100%

| 663kcal | 24g | 24g | 4g | 84g | 16g | 6g | 2g |
| CALORIES | PROTEIN | FAT | SAT FAT | CARBS | SUGAR | FIBRE | SALT |

PANEER KORMA

You can use the broccoli rice with other recipes if you wish.

CURRY

2 tablespoons **rapeseed oil**

1 **onion**, sliced

3 cloves **garlic**, chopped

200g **paneer cheese**, cut into cubes

1 medium **butternut squash**, peeled and cut into small chunks

3 tablespoons **Korma curry paste**

400ml tin **coconut milk**

4 tablespoons **ground almonds**

½ mug (150ml) **water**

1 mug (250g) **basmati rice**

1 head **broccoli**

1 Heat the oil in a large frying pan or wok. Add the onions and garlic and fry for 2–3 minutes.

2 Add the cheese and fry for 2 minutes.

3 Add the rest of the curry ingredients and bring to the boil. Season with salt and pepper. Simmer for 10 minutes with a lid on the pan. Stir every now and then.

4 Put the rice in a saucepan with 2 mugs of boiling water. Bring to the boil and simmer gently, with a lid on the pan, for 5 minutes.

5 Put the broccoli in the food processor and blitz until it looks like breadcrumbs. Add to the rice pan, don't stir, and simmer for a further 5 minutes, with the lid on the pan.

6 Stir the rice and broccoli together and serve with the curry.

RDA 100%

| 632kcal | 22g | 37g | 19g | 64g | 20g | 10g | 2g |
| CALORIES | PROTEIN | FAT | SAT FAT | CARBS | SUGAR | FIBRE | SALT |

HONEY TOFU AND QUINOA SALAD

Marinating the tofu enfuses it with flavour and the honey browns and caramelises it really nicely. Use raw honey if at all possible (see p 7).

GLUTEN-FREE OPTION: use GF soy sauce.

---

2 x 280g packets **firm tofu**, sliced

2 tablespoons **soy sauce**

2 tablespoons **runny honey**

2 tablespoons **toasted sesame oil**

½ mug (125g) **uncooked quinoa**

1 mug (300ml) boiling **water**

1 ½ mugs (200g) **frozen soy beans**, defrosted

250g **pomegranate seeds**

1 bunch **spring onions**, chopped

DRESSING

juice of a **lemon**

2 tablespoons **honey**

2 tablespoons **extra virgin olive oil**

1 tablespoon **toasted sesame oil**

1 Cut the tofu into slices and put in a bowl with the soy, honey and sesame oil. Leave to marinate for 10 minutes.

2 Put the quinoa in the boiling water and simmer for 12 minutes.

3 Add the beans and simmer for a further 2 minutes. Drain if necessary. Add the pomegranate seeds, onions and dressing. Season with salt and pepper.

4 Heat the other tablespoon of sesame oil in a frying pan and fry the drained tofu until browned. Add the tofu marinade and fry on a high heat for 2 minutes, taking care not to burn.

5 Serve the tofu on top of the quinoa salad and pour the sauce from the pan over each plate.

RDA 100%

596kcal	29g	33g	5g	41g	28g	9g	3g
CALORIES	PROTEIN	FAT	SAT FAT	CARBS	SUGAR	FIBRE	SALT

RICOTTA FRITTERS WITH CHUNKY CHILLI BEANS

These fritters are like delecate little 'pillows' of cheesiness. They are amazing.

GLUTEN-FREE OPTION: use GF flour and stock cubes.

CHILLI BEANS

1 tablespoon **olive oil**

1 **red onion**, chopped

3 cloves **garlic**, chopped

250g **chestnut mushrooms**, chopped

400g tin **red kidney beans**, drained and rinsed

2 **fat red chillies**

6 **tomatoes**, chopped

2 tablespoons **tomato purée**

1 **veg stock cube**

FRITTERS

2 **eggs**

400g **ricotta cheese**

²/₃ mug (40g) grated **Parmesan-style cheese**

6 tablespoons **self-raising flour**

oil to fry

1 Heat the oil in a frying pan and add the onions and garlic. Fry until the onion begins to soften.

2 Add the mushrooms and fry for 2–3 minutes.

3 Add the rest of the chilli bean ingredients and simmer for 2–3 minutes.

4 Mix together the fritter ingredients in a large bowl. Season with salt and pepper.

5 Heat the oil in a large frying pan and add 2 tablespoons of the mixture per fritter. Fry gently on a medium heat until the fritters brown lightly on both sides. The fritters should still be quite soft in the middle.

6 Serve with the chilli beans.

RDA 100%

| 433kcal | 22g | 21g | 11g | 36g | 14g | 7g | 1g |
| CALORIES | PROTEIN | FAT | SAT FAT | CARBS | SUGAR | FIBRE | SALT |

£ 1.55 /PERSON · SERVES 4 · EASE ★★☆☆☆ · PREP 20 MINS · GF OPTION

DOLCELATTE PASTA

I had not used Dolcelatte cheese very much before writing this book, but it is now creeping into lots of new recipes owing to its bold flavour.

GLUTEN-FREE OPTION: use GF pasta and stock cubes.

3 mugs (300g) **pasta**

2 tablespoons **olive oil**

2 **red onions**, sliced

1 clove **garlic**, chopped

300g **cherry tomatoes**, halved

6 **sun-dried tomatoes**, chopped

250g **mushrooms**, sliced

1 **veg stock cube**

1 tablespoon **tomato purée**

250g **Dolcelatte cheese**, cut into chunks

1 Put the pasta in a pan of boiling, salted water. Simmer for 10 minutes, retain ½ mug of the cooking liquid, drain the pasta and return to the pan.

2 Meanwhile, heat the oil in a frying pan and add the onions and garlic. Fry until the onions begin to soften. Season well with salt and pepper.

3 Add the tomatoes, sundried tomatoes and mushrooms and fry for 3–4 minutes.

4 Add the pasta water, stock cube and tomato purée and simmer for 1 minute.

5 Add the cheese and cooked pasta and gently stir; the cheese will melt into the mixture.

RDA 100%

| 498kcal | 17g | 30g | 16g | 38g | 9g | 5g | 2g |
| CALORIES | PROTEIN | FAT | SAT FAT | CARBS | SUGAR | FIBRE | SALT |

   GF OPTION Ve OPTION

HOT AND SOUR SOUP

If you have ever wondered (although you might not have) how you are meant to eat a noodle soup like this, it's easy. Just eat the noodles, and the vegetables, first and then drink the broth from the bowl. Don't worry if anyone says it's bad manners, you can just say we told you it was the traditional way to eat it!

VEGAN OPTION: use maple syrup instead of honey.

GLUTEN-FREE OPTION: use GF soy sauce and stock cubes.

100g **rice noodles**

2 tablespoons **toasted sesame oil**

4 **spring onions**, chopped

1 **red pepper**, sliced

2 cloves **garlic**, chopped

1 tablespoon freshly grated **ginger**

1 **fat red chilli**, chopped

5 mugs (1500ml) **water**

3 **veg stock cubes**

3 tablespoons **soy sauce**

1 tablespoon **mirin rice wine vinegar**

225g tin **bamboo shoots**, drained

1 teaspoon **honey**

250g **shiitake mushrooms**, sliced

100g **mangetout**, sliced

2 tablespoons freshly chopped **coriander**

1 Put the noodles in a large bowl of boiling water and leave to soak for 10 minutes. Drain and rinse and set to one side until needed.

2 Heat the oil in a wok or large saucepan. Add the onions, peppers, garlic, ginger and chilli. Fry for 2 minutes.

3 Add the water, stock, soy, mirin, bamboo shoots and honey and bring to the boil. Simmer for 2 minutes.

4 Add the mushrooms, mangetout and simmer for 1 minute.

5 Add the drained noodles to the pan.

6 Add the coriander and stir.

RDA 100%

257kcal	9g	8g	1g	33g	10g	6g	2g
CALORIES	PROTEIN	FAT	SAT FAT	CARBS	SUGAR	FIBRE	SALT

SATAY TOFU NOODLES

VEGAN OPTION: use maple syrup instead of honey.

GLUTEN-FREE OPTION: use GF soy sauce and stock cubes.

SATAY SAUCE

120g **peanut butter** (see p218)

250ml **coconut cream**

⅓ mug (100ml) **water**

1 **veg stock cube**

6 tablespoons **soy sauce**

1 tablespoon **honey**

1 tablespoon freshly grated **ginger**

1 **onion**, quartered

juice of ½ **lemon**

200g **dried rice noodles**

1 tablespoon **toasted sesame oil**

280g **firm tofu**, cut into bite-sized pieces

1 **red pepper**, chopped

1 **fat red chilli**, chopped

250g **mushrooms**, sliced

2 tablespoons freshly chopped **coriander**

1 Put the satay sauce ingredients in a blender and blitz until smooth.

2 Put the noodles in a large bowl and cover with boiling water, leaving to stand for 10 minutes. Drain and rinse and set to one side until needed.

3 Meanwhile, heat the sesame oil in a large frying pan. Add the tofu and fry until it is browned.

4 Add the peppers, chilli and mushrooms to the pan and fry for 3–4 minutes, or until they begin to brown a little.

5 Add the satay sauce to the pan and bring to the boil. Allow to simmer for 2 minutes.

6 Serve on the drained noodles. Garnish with the chopped coriander.

RDA 100%

682kcal	28g	36g	16g	58g	14g	6g	5g
CALORIES	PROTEIN	FAT	SAT FAT	CARBS	SUGAR	FIBRE	SALT

£1.25 /PERSON · SERVES 4 · EASE ★★★☆☆ · PREP 20 MINS · COOK 50 MINS · GF OPTION

BEETROOT BURGERS WITH HONEY PARSNIPS

GLUTEN-FREE OPTION: use GF bread.

6 **parsnips**, peeled and halved

1 tablespoon **olive oil**

2 tablespoons **runny honey**

400g tin **cannellini beans**, drained and rinsed

2 slices **bread**

1 **red onion**, quartered

500g **raw beetroot**, peeled

1 **egg yolk**

2 tablespoons **miso paste**

1 tablespoon **olive oil**

100g **kale**

1 Preheat the oven to 180°C/200°C/gas 6.

2 Put the parsnips on a roasting tray. Drizzle with the oil and season with salt and pepper. Mix everything together and spread out on the tray.

3 Roast in the oven for 40 minutes. Drizzle over the honey and roast for a further 10 minutes.

4 Meanwhile, make the burgers. Put the drained beans in a processor, with the bread and onion, and blitz.

5 Put the grating blade on the processor and grate the beetroot.

6 Tip out into a bowl and mix together with the egg yolk and miso. Season with salt and pepper. Form into 8 small burgers.

7 Heat the oil in a frying pan and fry the burgers on a medium heat, until they are cooked through and browned lightly on each side. You may need to do this in two batches.

8 Put the kale in a large saucepan or wok. Add ¼ mug water. Simmer for 3-4 minutes with a lid on the pan.

9 Serve the burgers with the parsnips and kale.

RDA 100%

404kcal	15g	12g	2g	52g	29g	14g	2g
CALORIES	PROTEIN	FAT	SAT FAT	CARBS	SUGAR	FIBRE	SALT

SAAG ALOO AND PANEER MADRAS

You almost have two dishes in one here, but we have tried to keep both of them as simple as possible.

2 tablespoons **olive oil**

2 **onions**, sliced

2 cloves **garlic**, chopped

225g **paneer cheese**, cut into cubes

6 **tomatoes**, chopped

2 tablespoons **Madras curry paste**

2 mugs (300g) **frozen peas**, defrosted

2 tablespoons freshly chopped **coriander**

6 medium **potatoes**, cut into chunks

3 tablespoons **olive oil**

1 **onion**, sliced

1 clove **garlic**, chopped

1 tablespoon freshly grated **ginger**

1 tablespoon **cumin seeds**

1 tablespoon **black mustard seeds**

2 teaspoons **ground coriander**

2 teaspoons **garam masala**

200g **spinach**

1 Make the curry. Heat the oil in a large frying pan. Add the onions, garlic and paneer and fry until things begin to brown.

2 Add the tomatoes and curry paste and cook for 2–3 minutes.

3 Add the peas and heat through. Add the coriander just before serving.

4 To make the Saag Aloo, put the potatoes in a pan of boiling, salted water and simmer for 8 minutes. Drain and return to the pan.

5 Meanwhile, heat the oil in a large frying pan or wok. Add the onions, garlic and ginger and fry until the onions begin to brown.

6 Add the seeds and spices and fry for 2 minutes, stirring frequently. Season well with salt and pepper.

7 Add the potatoes to the pan and fry for 2 minutes.

8 Add the spinach and cook until the spinach just wilts.

9 Serve with the curry.

RDA 100%

| 738kcal | 25g | 32g | 9g | 80g | 19g | 14g | 1g |
| CALORIES | PROTEIN | FAT | SAT FAT | CARBS | SUGAR | FIBRE | SALT |

LENTIL BALLS

GLUTEN-FREE OPTION: use GF bread.

LENTIL BALLS

2 slices **bread**

½ mug (100g) **cashew nuts**

1 **red onion**, peeled and quartered

2 cloves **garlic**

400g tin **green lentils**, drained and rinsed

½ x 400g tin **pinto beans**, drained and rinsed

1 **egg**

¼ mug (15g) finely grated, **Parmesan-style cheese**

1 teaspoon **paprika**

salt and **pepper**

400g **spaghetti**

TOMATO SAUCE

1 tablespoon **olive oil**

1 **red onion**, sliced

3 cloves **garlic**, chopped

6 **tomatoes**

1 tablespoon **cornflour**

2 tablespoons **tomato purée**

3 tablespoons freshly chopped **basil**

salt and **pepper**

1 Preheat the oven to 180°C fan/200°C/ gas 6. Line a baking tray.

2 Put the bread, nuts, onion, and garlic in a food processor and blitz. Add the rest of the lentil ball ingredients and blitz again.

3 Form the mixture into 20 balls and place on the baking tray. Bake in the oven for 30 minutes.

4 15 minutes before the end of the cooking time, put the spaghetti in a saucepan of boiling salted water. Simmer for 10 minutes. Drain and return to the pan.

5 Heat a little oil in a saucepan and fry the onions and garlic. Put these, along with the rest of the tomato sauce ingredients, in a blender and blitz until smooth. Pour back into the saucepan and simmer for 5 minutes.

6 Serve the meatballs on top of the spaghetti and pour over the sauce.

RDA 100%

582kcal	21g	21g	5g	71g	11g	11g	0.5g
CALORIES	PROTEIN	FAT	SAT FAT	CARBS	SUGAR	FIBRE	SALT

£2.02 /PERSON · SERVES 4 · EASE ★★★☆☆ · PREP 20 MINS · COOK 45 MINS · GF

ROAST BUTTERNUT WITH PISTACHIO HUMMUS

Don't be tempted to buy the hummus instead of making this one. Pistachio hummus is like no hummus you have tried before (unless you have tried pistachio hummus of course!).

1 medium **butternut squash**, peeled and cut into chunks

2 **red onions**, peeled and cut into wedges

4 cloves **garlic**, left whole

250g **chestnut mushrooms**, halved

400g tin **cannellini beans**, drained and rinsed

3 tablespoons **olive oil**

2 tablespoons **balsamic vinegar**

200g **cherry tomatoes**

HUMMUS

²/₃ mug (100g) **pistachios**

200g **feta**

400g tin **chickpeas**, drained and rinsed

juice of a **lemon**

3 tablespoons **Greek yogurt**

1 Preheat the oven to 200°C fan/220°C/gas 7.

2 Put the vegetables and beans, but not the tomatoes, on a large roasting tray.

3 Drizzle with the oil and season well with salt and pepper. Mix together and spread out evenly on the tray. Drizzle over the balsamic vinegar. Roast in the oven for 35 minutes. Add the tomatoes and cook for a further 10 minutes.

4 Put the hummus ingredients in a food processor, season with salt and pepper and blitz until smooth.

5 Divide the hummus between the plates and spread a little. Serve the hot roasted veg on top. Enjoy.

120

RDA 100%

703kcal	29g	37g	12g	57g	22g	23g	4g
CALORIES	PROTEIN	FAT	SAT FAT	CARBS	SUGAR	FIBRE	SALT

MUSHROOM AND CHESTNUT PIE

The mushroom-shaped pastry on top of the pie might not be essential, but what else are you going to do with the trimmings? Go on, live a little, have some fun!

360g **plain flour**

1/2 teaspoon **salt**

175g cold **butter**

1 **egg** + 75ml cold **water**

3 tablespoons **olive oil**

2 **onions**, sliced

3 cloves **garlic**, sliced

500g **chestnut mushrooms**, sliced

200g **whole cooked chestnuts**, roughly chopped

1 tablespoon **plain flour**

2 sprigs **rosemary leaves**, chopped

1 teaspoon **coconut sugar**

300ml **vegetarian cider**

1 **veg stock cube**

2 tablespoons **soy sauce**

200g **cavalo nero**, chopped

1 To make the pastry, put the flour, salt and butter in a food processor and blitz until you have something resembling breadcrumbs. Add the egg and water and pulse a few times.

2 Take out of the processor, press together, cover with cling film and leave in the fridge until needed.

3 Preheat the oven to 180°C fan/200°C/gas 6.

4 Heat the oil in a large frying pan. Add the onions and garlic and fry for 2-3 minutes.

5 Add the mushrooms and chestnuts and fry for 3-4 minutes. Add the flour and mix.

6 Add the rosemary, sugar, cider, stock cube and soy sauce. Season with salt and pepper. Bring to the boil and the sauce should thicken.

7 Pour the contents of the pan into a large casserole dish.

8 Roll out the pastry and lay over the top and brush with beaten egg. Bake in the oven for 35 minutes.

9 5 minutes before the end of the cooking time, put the cavalo nero in a pan of boiling, salted water. Simmer for 3 minutes. Drain and return to the pan.

RDA 100%

| 786kcal | 17g | 41g | 20g | 78g | 14g | 7g | 2g |
| CALORIES | PROTEIN | FAT | SAT FAT | CARBS | SUGAR | FIBRE | SALT |

CURRIED COURGETTE BALLS

Sweet coconutty sauce to accompany lightly spiced, courgette balls.

SAUCE

1 tablespoon **olive oil**

2 **onions**, chopped

4 **tomatoes**, chopped

2 tablespoons **korma curry paste**

400ml tin **coconut milk**

1 tablespoon **cornflour**

1 ½ mugs (375g) **basmati rice**

COURGETTE BALLS

4 **courgettes**, grated

1 tablespoon freshly grated **ginger**

2 tablespoons freshly chopped **coriander**

4 tablespoons **garam flour**

salt and **pepper**

2 tablespoons **olive oil**

1 Heat the oil in a saucepan and fry the onions for 2–3 minutes. Put in a blender with the rest of the ingredients for the sauce and blitz until smooth. Pour back into the saucepan and bring to the boil. Simmer for 2 minutes.

2 Put the rice in a saucepan with 3 mugs of boiling water. Bring to the boil and simmer gently, with a lid on the pan, for 10 minutes.

3 Mix the courgette ball ingredients together in a bowl. Divide into 12 balls.

4 Heat the oil in a pan and fry the courgette balls until they are nicely browned on all sides.

5 Serve with the rice and the sauce.

RDA 100%

479kcal	10g	28g	14g	62g	14g	5g	0.5g
CALORIES	PROTEIN	FAT	SAT FAT	CARBS	SUGAR	FIBRE	SALT

HALLOUMI FRITTERS

Halloumi has a great flavour on its own. Here it has the additional element of caramelisation - delicious!

GLUTEN-FREE OPTION: use GF bread.

4 **sweet potatoes,** peeled and cut into wedges

2 tablespoons **olive oil**

FRITTERS

2 x 250g packets **halloumi**, grated

1 **red onion**, grated. Squeeze out the excess liquid.

2 cloves **garlic**, chopped

zest of a **lemon**

1 **fat red chilli**, finely chopped

2 slices **bread**, made into breadcrumbs

2 tablespoons freshly chopped **basil**

3 **eggs**, beaten

2 tablespoons **olive oil**

SAUCE

6 tablespoons **Greek yogurt**

juice of ½ **lemon**

2 tablespoons freshly chopped **mint**

½ **cucumber**, grated. Squeeze out the excess liquid.

1 Preheat the oven to 180°C fan/200°C/ gas 6.

2 Put the sweet potato wedges on a large roasting tray, along with the oil. Mix everything together, season well with salt and pepper, and spread out evenly. Roast in the oven for 40 minutes.

3 20 minutes before the sweet potatoes are ready, put the fritter ingredients in a large bowl, season with salt and pepper, and mix together.

4 Heat the oil in a large frying pan and form small handfuls of the mixture. Place into the pan, this should make about 20 fritters. Fry on each side until lightly browned. Keep them warm if you need to fry in batches.

5 Serve with the combined sauce ingredients to one side.

you can reduce this number by using 'low-fat' halloumi

RDA 100%

949kcal	43g	55g	28g	67g	21g	8g	4g
CALORIES	PROTEIN	FAT	SAT FAT	CARBS	SUGAR	FIBRE	SALT

MUSHROOM STROGANOFF

Quick and easy to make. Ideal when you have a busy day.

VEGAN OPTION: use olive oil instead of butter.

GLUTEN-FREE OPTION: use GF pasta and stock cubes.

300g **linguine**

1 tablespoon **olive oil**

2 **red onions**, sliced

3 cloves **garlic**, chopped

500g **chestnut mushrooms**, sliced

300ml **crème fraîche**

1 tablespoon **smoked paprika**

1 **veg stock cube**

1 tablespoon **Dijon mustard**

3 tablespoons freshly chopped **chives**

1 Put the linguine in a large saucepan with plenty of boiling water. Bring to the boil and then simmer for 10 minutes. Drain and return to the pan.

2 Meanwhile, heat the butter in a large frying pan or wok. Add the onions and garlic and fry for 3–4 minutes, or until the onions begin to brown a little.

3 Add the mushrooms and fry for 2–3 minutes.

4 Add the rest of the ingredients (keep some chives to garnish at the end) and bring to the boil. Season well with salt and pepper and simmer for 3 minutes.

5 Stir in the drained linguine and serve.

RDA 100%

577kcal	15g	29g	17g	61g	9g	5g	1g
CALORIES	PROTEIN	FAT	SAT FAT	CARBS	SUGAR	FIBRE	SALT

£2.05 /PERSON · SERVES 4 · EASE ★★☆☆☆ · PREP 15 MINS · COOK 25 MINS · GF OPTION

GNOCCHI BAKE

We have never really had gnocchi in a bake before. We are certainly not claiming to have invented it, but if you have not tried it before, give it a go.

GLUTEN-FREE OPTION: use GF gnocchi.

---

1 bunch **spring onions**, chopped

500g **cherry tomatoes**, halved

200g **spinach**, roughly chopped

400g tin **butter beans**, drained and rinsed

½ mug (150ml) **water**

2 tablespoons **sun-dried tomato purée**

500g **gnocchi**

125g **mozzarella**, torn up

1 Preheat the oven to 180°C fan/200°C/gas 6.

2 In a large bowl, mix together the spring onions, tomatoes, spinach, beans, water and sun-dried tomatoes. Gently mix in the gnocchi. Season well with salt and pepper.

3 Pour into the casserole dish. Add the mozzarella over the top.

4 Bake in the oven for 25 minutes.

RDA 100%

400kcal	15g	10g	5g	61g	8g	10g	2g
CALORIES	PROTEIN	FAT	SAT FAT	CARBS	SUGAR	FIBRE	SALT

CHICKPEA CURRY

Using nut butters in sauces is a great idea. Here it blends perfectly with the tomato and coconut milk.

GLUTEN-FREE OPTION: use GF stock cubes.

1 ½ mugs (375g) **basmati rice**

2 tablespoons **toasted sesame oil**

365g pack **firm tofu**, cut into cubes

2 **onions**, chopped

2 cloves **garlic**, chopped

1 **fat red chilli**, chopped

2 tablespoons freshly grated **ginger**

1 **veg stock cube**, crumbled

2 tablespoons **garam masala**

1 tablespoon **cumin**

1 tablespoon **ground coriander**

400g tin **chickpeas**, rinsed and drained

SAUCE

120g **cashew nut butter** (see p218)

400ml tin **coconut milk**

2 tablespoons **tomato purée**

2 tablespoons **coconut sugar**

juice of ½ **lemon**

1 Put the rice in a saucepan with 3 mugs of boiling water. Bring to the boil and simmer gently, with a lid on the pan, for 10 minutes.

2 Meanwhile, heat the sesame oil in a large frying pan. Add the tofu, onions, and garlic and fry until everything browns.

3 Add the chilli and ginger to the pan and fry for 2 minutes.

4 Add the stock cube, garam masala, cumin, coriander and chickpeas. Fry for 1 minute.

5 Combine the sauce ingredients and add to the pan. Season well with salt and pepper. Bring to the boil. Simmer for 4–5 minutes.

6 Serve with the rice.

RDA 100%

758kcal	30g	46g	17g	76g	15g	7g	1g
CALORIES	PROTEIN	FAT	SAT FAT	CARBS	SUGAR	FIBRE	SALT

ROAST AUBERGINE CIABATTA

Aubergines can be quite bland, but, once roasted, the flavours are wonderfully transformed. If possible, use cold-pressed, organic, rapeseed oil.

GLUTEN-FREE OPTION: use GF bread.

---

2 **aubergines**, sliced lengthways

2 tablespoons **rapeseed oil**

250g **mozzarella**, sliced

1 tablespoon **rapeseed oil**

1 **red onion**, sliced

1 clove **garlic**, chopped

6 **tomatoes**, chopped

1 tablespoon **tomato purée**

1 tablespoon **balsamic vinegar**

zest of a **lemon**

2 tablespoons freshly chopped **basil**

1 large **ciabatta**

1 Preheat the oven to 180°C fan/200°C/gas 6.

2 Put the aubergine slices on the tray and drizzle with the oil. Season well with salt and pepper and mix everything together. Space out on the tray and roast in the oven for 25 minutes.

3 Once the aubergines are cooked, take out of the oven, place the mozzarella on top of each slice, and return to the oven for 10 minutes.

4 Meanwhile, make the sauce. Heat the oil in a large saucepan, add the onion and garlic and fry for 3–4 minutes.

5 Add the tomatoes and fry for a further 2 minutes. Add the tomato purée and balsamic and take off the heat. Set to one side until needed.

6 Take the aubergines out of the oven and sprinkle with the lemon zest and basil.

7 Cut the ciabatta into 4 and put the sauce on top, followed by the aubergines.

RDA 100%

573kcal	23g	27g	10g	56g	14g	7g	1g
CALORIES	PROTEIN	FAT	SAT FAT	CARBS	SUGAR	FIBRE	SALT

BRIE SOUFFLÉ WITH ROAST BEETS

GLUTEN-FREE OPTION: use GF flour.

500g **raw beetroot**, peeled and cut into wedges

2 **red onions**, cut into wedges

2 tablespoons **olive oil**

50g **butter**, measure using packet

35g **plain flour**

500ml **milk**

100ml **double cream**

5 **eggs**, separated

300g **brie**, chopped

1 tablespoon **wholegrain mustard**

bag **rocket salad**

DRESSING

1 tablespoon **cider vinegar**

1 tablespoon **maple syrup**

1 tablespoon **extra virgin olive oil**

1 Preheat the oven to 180°C fan/200°C/gas 6. Grease 4 ramekins with some butter and place on a baking tray.

2 Put the beetroot and onions on a roasting tray and drizzle with the oil. Season with salt and pepper and mix everything together. Spread out on the tray and roast in the oven for 45 minutes.

3 Heat the 50g of butter in a large saucepan, add the flour and mix together. Add the milk and cream and bring to the boil. Stir frequently, the sauce will thicken. Remove from the heat and leave to cool for 5 minutes.

4 Separate the eggs, putting the yolks in the sauce and the whites in a large bowl.

5 Add the cheese and mustard to the sauce, mix well and season with salt and pepper.

6 Beat the egg whites until they form soft peaks. Gently fold into the sauce.

7 Divide the mixture between the ramekins. Bake in the oven for 25 minutes until nicely browned. Don't open the oven early as they might collapse.

8 Serve with the roasted beets, onions, rocket and combined dressing ingredients.

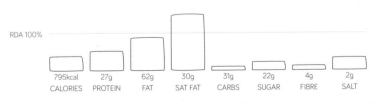

RDA 100%

795kcal	27g	62g	30g	31g	22g	4g	2g
CALORIES	PROTEIN	FAT	SAT FAT	CARBS	SUGAR	FIBRE	SALT

£1.09 /PERSON · SERVES 4 · EASE ★★★☆☆ · PREP 25 MINS · COOK 50 MINS · GF OPTION · Ve OPTION

ROAST SQUASH WITH ALMOND BUTTER SAUCE

Making different kinds of nut butters is really easy. They will keep in sealed jars for months.

VEGAN OPTION: use vegan margarine instead of butter.

GLUTEN-FREE OPTION: use GF stock cubes.

4 medium **potatoes**, cut into chunks

1 **butternut squash**, peeled and cut into wedges

4 cloves **garlic**, sliced

2 tablespoons **olive oil**

SAUCE

2 tablespoons **olive oil**

1 **onion**, chopped

1 **fat red chilli**, chopped

juice of a **lemon**

1 mug (300ml) **water**

1 **veg stock cube**

4 tablespoons **almond butter** (see p218)

3 mugs (450g) **frozen peas**, defrosted

25g **butter**, measure using packet

1 Preheat the oven to 180°C fan/200°C/gas 6.

2 Put the potatoes, squash and garlic on a roasting tray, drizzle with the oil, season well with salt and pepper, and mix everything together. Spread out and roast in the oven for 50 minutes, or until browned.

3 To make the sauce, heat the oil in a frying pan and fry the onion until it begins to brown. Add the chilli and fry for 1 minute.

4 Add the rest of the sauce ingredients and stir well. Bring to the boil and simmer for 1 minute.

5 5 minutes before the end of the roasting time for the potatoes, put the peas in a saucepan of boiling water, simmer for 1 minute and then drain. Return to the pan and add the butter. Mash and serve with the squash, potatoes and the sauce.

RDA 100%

| 682kcal | 19g | 32g | 6g | 72g | 19g | 15g | 0.2g |
| CALORIES | PROTEIN | FAT | SAT FAT | CARBS | SUGAR | FIBRE | SALT |

THAI RICE WITH STIR-FRY GREENS

Cooking rice in coconut mlk is always a winner. Adding the egg takes it to another level.

VEGAN OPTION: use maple syrup instead of honey.

GLUTEN-FREE OPTION: use GF soy sauce.

THAI RICE

1 mug (250g) **basmati rice**
400ml tin **coconut milk**
4 **eggs**, beaten
3 tablespoons **soy sauce**
1 mug (200g) **cashew nuts**

STIR-FRY

2 tablespoons **coconut oil**
2 **pak choi**, sliced
1 bunch **spring onions**, sliced
200g **sugar snaps**, sliced
1 mug (150g) **frozen peas**, defrosted
250g **chestnut mushrooms**, sliced

SAUCE

juice of a **lime**
1 tablespoon **honey**
1 **fat red chilli**, sliced

1 Put the rice into a saucepan, with the coconut milk, and 1 mug of boiling water. Bring to the boil and simmer gently, with a lid on the pan, for 10 minutes.

2 Mix the rest of the rice ingredients and add to the cooked rice. Stir a little and leave the lid on until needed. The heat of the pan should cook the egg.

3 Heat the coconut oil in a wok. Add the stir-fry ingredients and cook on a high heat for 2 minutes.

4 Mix together the sauce ingredients and add to the wok. Heat for 1 minute.

5 Serve on the rice.

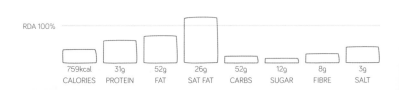

RDA 100%

| 759kcal | 31g | 52g | 26g | 52g | 12g | 8g | 3g |
| CALORIES | PROTEIN | FAT | SAT FAT | CARBS | SUGAR | FIBRE | SALT |

£1.63 /PERSON · SERVES 4 · EASE ★★☆☆☆ · PREP 20 MINS · COOK 50 MINS · GF

MANCHEGO WEDGES WITH CELERIAC SALAD

Nothing like the 'cheesy chips' you get from burger vans, but just as moreish.

8 medium **potatoes**, cut into wedges

2 tablespoons **rapeseed oil**

200g **manchego cheese**, grated

CELERIAC SALAD

1 small (400g) **celeriac**, grated

2 tablespoons freshly chopped **coriander**

1 tablespoon freshly chopped **parsley**

2 tablespoons **extra virgin olive oil**

½ mug (100g) **peanuts**, roughly chopped

juice of a **lemon**

salt and **pepper**

chilli jam (see p217)

1 Preheat the oven to 180°C fan/200°C/gas 6.

2 Put the potato wedges on a roasting tray. Season with salt and pepper. Drizzle over the oil, mix everything together and then spread out evenly. Roast in the oven for 50 minutes, or until browned.

3 Remove from the oven and add the cheese over the top, to melt. Return to the oven for a minute or so, just to melt slightly.

4 Meanwhile, mix together the celeriac salad ingredients in a large bowl.

5 Serve with the wedges and the chilli jam.

RDA 100%

| 835kcal | 27g | 46g | 18g | 73g | 8g | 11g | 2g |
| CALORIES | PROTEIN | FAT | SAT FAT | CARBS | SUGAR | FIBRE | SALT |

BOURSIN CHEESE PARCELS

Crunchy parcels of savoury goodness topped with sharpness from the salsa verde.

GLUTEN-FREE OPTION: use GF pastry.

---

5 medium **potatoes**, cut into chunks

2 tablespoons **olive oil**

2 tablespoons **olive oil**

3 **red onions**, sliced

150g **Boursin cheese**

½ mug (100g) **pine nuts**

1 sheet **ready-made puff pastry**

1 **egg**, beaten

1 tablespoon **sesame seeds**

salsa verde, make your own (see p215)

1 Preheat the oven to 200°C fan/220°C/gas 7.

2 Put the potatoes on a roasting tray and drizzle with the first two tablespoons of the oil. Season with salt and pepper, mix together and spread the out potatoes. Roast in the oven for 45 minutes, or until browned.

3 Heat the other two tablespoons of oil in a frying pan and add the onions. Season well with salt and pepper. Fry on a medium heat until the onions begin to caramelise. Take off the heat and allow to cool.

4 Mix the Boursin and pine nuts with the caramelised onions.

5 Unroll the pastry and cut into 4 pieces. Divide the onion filling between the pieces. Wet the edges and fold over the pastry (see photo). Place on a greased and lined baking tray.

6 Brush with beaten egg. Sprinkle over the sesame seeds. Bake in the oven for 20–25 minutes. The parcels should be lightly browned.

7 Meanwhile, make the salsa verde and serve everything together.

144

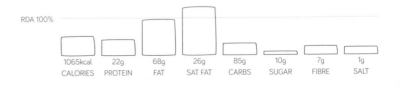

RDA 100%

1065kcal	22g	68g	26g	85g	10g	7g	1g
CALORIES	PROTEIN	FAT	SAT FAT	CARBS	SUGAR	FIBRE	SALT

£2.36 /PERSON — SERVES 4 — EASE ★★☆☆☆ — PREP 20 MINS — GF OPTION — Ve

MIXED MUSHROOM RISOTTO

Make sure the risotto stays creamy. Add more water if it goes a little dry.

GLUTEN-FREE OPTION: use GF stock cubes.

2 tablespoons **olive oil**	**1** Heat the oil in a large frying pan or wok. Add the onion and fry until it begins to soften.
1 **red onion**, sliced	
2 cloves **garlic**, chopped	**2** Add the garlic and mushrooms and fry for 2–3 minutes.
150g **chestnut mushrooms**, sliced	
250g **mixed mushrooms**, sliced	**3** Add the rice and fry for 30 seconds.
1 mug (215g) **risotto rice**	**4** Add the coconut milk, water and stock cube and bring to the boil.
400ml tin **coconut milk**	
²/₃ mug (200ml) **water**	**5** Season well with salt and pepper and simmer for 10 minutes with a lid on the pan.
1 **veg stock cube**	
juice of a **lime**	**6** Add the lime juice and coriander and serve with the cashews sprinkled on top.
3 tablespoons freshly chopped **coriander**	
1 mug (200g) **cashew nuts**	

RDA 100%

689kcal	17g	45g	18g	52g	5g	4g	1g
CALORIES	PROTEIN	FAT	SAT FAT	CARBS	SUGAR	FIBRE	SALT

£ 1.32 /PERSON · SERVES 4 · EASE ★★★☆☆ · PREP 25 MINS · COOK 50 MINS · GF OPTION · Ve OPTION

AUBERGINE DHAL WITH ROAST VEG

VEGAN OPTION: use vegan margarine instead of butter.

GLUTEN-FREE OPTION: use GF stock cubes.

2 **carrots**, peeled and cut into sticks

1 **onion**, cut into wedges

2 **parsnips**, peeled and cut into sticks

2 tablespoons **rapeseed oil**

1 tablespoon **pomegranate molasses**

DHAL

25g **butter**, measure using packet

2 **onions**, chopped

1 **aubergine**, chopped

2 teaspoons **garam masala**

2 teaspoons **turmeric**

3 cloves **garlic**, chopped

2 tablespoons freshly grated **ginger**

6 **tomatoes**, chopped

1 **fat green chilli**, chopped

1 mug (300ml) **water**

1 **veg stock cube**

400g tin **green lentils**, drained and rinsed

1 ½ mugs (375g) **basmati rice**

1 Preheat the oven to 180°C fan/200°C/ gas 6. Put the carrots, onions and parsnips in a roasting tray. Drizzle with the oil and season well with salt and pepper. Roast in the oven for 50 minutes. Drizzle with the pomegranate molasses and mix.

2 20 minutes before the end of the cooking time for the roast veggies, make the dhal. Heat the butter in a large saucepan or wok. Add the onions and aubergines and fry for 5 minutes.

3 Add the spices, garlic and ginger and fry for 2 minutes. Season well.

4 Add the tomatoes and chilli and fry for a further 3 minutes.

5 Add the rest of the dhal ingredients, apart from the coriander, and simmer for 10 minutes.

6 Put the rice in a pan with 3 mugs of boiling water. Bring to the boil and simmer gently, with a lid on the pan, for 10 minutes.

7 Serve the dhal with the rice and veg.

RDA 100%

461kcal	13g	16g	5g	82g	23g	13g	0.3g
CALORIES	PROTEIN	FAT	SAT FAT	CARBS	SUGAR	FIBRE	SALT

DOLCELATTE CAULIFLOWER FRITTERS

Once you have tried these fritters, you may never be tempted to make cauliflower cheese again. This is such a good way to cook cauliflower and cheese.

GLUTEN-FREE OPTION: use GF flour.

PISTACHIO DIP

²/₃ mug (100g) **pistachios**

250g **ricotta cheese**

100ml **Greek yogurt**

juice of a **lemon**

2 tablespoons freshly chopped **basil**

salt and **pepper**

1 small **cauliflower**, cut into small florets

1 mug (180g) **self-raising flour**

4 **eggs**

220g **Dolcelatte cheese**

3 tablespoons freshly chopped **basil**

4 tablespoons **rapeseed oil**

2 mugs (300g) **frozen peas**, defrosted

20g **butter**, measure using packet

1 To make the dip. Put the pistachios in a processor and blitz, but don't make them too fine. Add the rest of the dip ingredients and pulse a couple of times.

2 Put the cauliflower in a pan of boiling, salted water and simmer for 5 minutes.

3 Meanwhile, mix together the flour and eggs. Crumble the cheese and add along with the basil. Season well with salt and pepper.

4 Drain the cauliflower and add to the batter.

5 Heat the oil in a large frying pan. Add dollops of the mixture to the pan, it should make between 8 and 10 fritters. Fry until they are browned nicely on all sides.

6 To make the pea mash, put the peas in a pan of boiling water and simmer for 1 minute. Drain and return to the pan. Add the butter and then mash.

7 Serve the fritters with the pea mash and the dip.

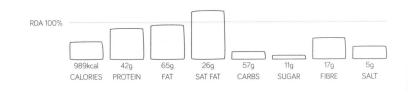

RDA 100%

989kcal	42g	65g	26g	57g	11g	17g	5g
CALORIES	PROTEIN	FAT	SAT FAT	CARBS	SUGAR	FIBRE	SALT

£3.12 /PERSON · SERVES 4 · EASE. ★★★☆☆ · PREP 25 MINS · COOK 25 MINS · GF OPTION

PESTO PUFF PASTRY TART

Using nut butter in the dressing, along with the apple juice, is quite unusual, but really effective. You can use this dressing with other salads.

GLUTEN-FREE OPTION: use GF pastry.

320g sheet **ready-rolled puff pastry**

50g **basil**

1/2 mug (100g) **pine nuts**

8 tablespoons **olive oil**

100g pack **Boursin**

20 **black olives**

200g **cherry tomatoes**, halved

2/3 mug (50g) grated **Cheddar cheese**

APPLE ALMOND AND DATE SALAD

1/2 mug (50g) **flaked almonds**

2 **Granny Smith apples**, sliced

10 **medjool dates**, de-stoned and sliced

1 **Romaine lettuce**, sliced

DRESSING

2 tablespoons **almond butter** (see p218)

3 tablespoons **extra virgin olive oil**

3 tablespoons **fresh apple juice**

juice of a **lemon**

1 Preheat the oven to 200°C fan/220°C/ gas 7. Grease a large baking tray.

2 Unroll the pastry and place on the baking sheet. Score a 2cm perimeter and prick the centre with a fork. Bake in the oven for 10 minutes.

3 To make the pesto, put the basil, pine nuts and olive oil in a blender and blitz.

4 After 10 minutes take the pastry out of the oven. Put 'blobs' of the Boursin evenly over the tart. Add the olives and tomatoes.

5 Sprinkle the Cheddar over. Add generous dollops of the pesto. Season well with salt and pepper.

6 Bake in the oven for a further 15 minutes. The crust should be nicely browned.

7 Meanwhile, combine the salad ingredients in a large bowl and mix in the combined dressing ingredients.

you can reduce these numbers by using 'light' puff pastry

RDA 100%

1307kcal CALORIES	23g PROTEIN	98g FAT	27g SAT FAT	77g CARBS	44g SUGAR	11g FIBRE	1g SALT

TOFU BALLS WITH PESTO PASTA

The tomato pesto can be used with other pasta dishes. Also, you could add other main ingredients, such as burgers, instead of the tofu.

GLUTEN-FREE OPTION: use GF pasta and bread.

TOFU BALLS

1 **onion**, chopped

3 cloves **garlic**

400g **firm tofu**

2 tablespoons freshly chopped **basil**

3 slices **bread**

½ mug (40g) grated **Cheddar cheese**

1 **egg**

SUN-DRIED TOMATO PESTO

120g **sun-dried tomatoes**

25g **fresh basil**

½ mug (100g) **pine nuts**

2 cloves **garlic**

4 tablespoons **extra virgin olive oil**

3 tablespoons **maple syrup**

juice of ½ **lemon**

3 mugs **pasta**

1   Preheat the oven to 180°C fan/200°C/gas 6. Grease a baking tray.

2   Put the tofu ball ingredients, apart from the egg, in a processor and blitz until you have something resembling breadcrumbs. Season well with salt and pepper.

3   Add the egg and pulse a few times. Take the mixture out of the processor and form into 20 balls. Place on the baking sheet and bake in the oven for 25 minutes.

4   Meanwhile, make the pesto. Simply put all the ingredients in a blender and blitz. Season with salt and pepper. Tip out into a small saucepan and heat gently for 5 minutes.

5   Put the pasta in a pan of boiling, salted water and simmer until tender. Drain and return to the pan. Add the pesto and stir.

6   Serve with the tofu balls.

RDA 100%

761kcal	31g	43g	7g	57g	15g	8g	2g
CALORIES	PROTEIN	FAT	SAT FAT	CARBS	SUGAR	FIBRE	SALT

CURRIED SWEET POTATO AND SPINACH GRATIN

Quite an unusual dish with layers of spinach, lentil curry and sweet potato.

GLUTEN-FREE OPTION: use GF naan breads.

1 tablespoon **olive oil**

1 **onion**, sliced

1 teaspoon **black mustard seeds**

3 cloves **garlic**, sliced

400g tin **green lentils**, drained and rinsed

1 **red chilli**, chopped

2 tablespoons **korma curry paste**

4 **tomatoes**, roughly chopped

2 x 400ml tin **coconut milk**

200g **spinach**, chopped

3 medium **sweet potatoes**, thinly sliced

4 **naan breads**

1 Preheat the oven to 180°C fan/200°C/gas 6. Grease a casserole.

2 Heat the oil in a saucepan. Add the onion and mustard seeds and cook gently, over a medium/low heat, until the onions begin to soften.

3 Stir in the garlic, lentils and chillies and cook for 2 minutes. Mix in the curry paste, tomatoes and coconut milk. Season well with salt and pepper and simmer for 5 minutes.

4 Spread the spinach across the base of a large casserole dish. Top with the lentil mixture, followed by the sweet potatoes. Drizzle with oil and season with salt and pepper.

5 Bake in the oven for 30 minutes, or until the potatoes are tender and browned slightly.

6 Serve with naan bread.

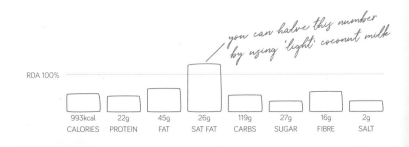

you can halve this number by using 'light' coconut milk

RDA 100%

993kcal	22g	45g	26g	119g	27g	16g	2g
CALORIES	PROTEIN	FAT	SAT FAT	CARBS	SUGAR	FIBRE	SALT

   GF OPTION Ve

COCONUT CHICKPEA CURRY

GLUTEN-FREE OPTION: use GF stock cubes.

1 ½ mugs (375g) **basmati rice**

2 tablespoons **rapeseed oil**

1 **onion**, chopped

1 large **sweet potato**, cut into small chunks

2 teaspoons **garam masala**

½ teaspoon **ground nutmeg**

250g **mushrooms**, sliced

400g tin **chickpeas**, drained and rinsed

400ml tin **coconut milk**

1 **veg stock cube**

3 tablespoons **green curry paste**

1 tablespoon freshly grated **ginger**

2 tablespoons freshly chopped **coriander**

1 Put the rice in a saucepan with 3 mugs of boiling water. Bring to the boil and simmer gently, with a lid on the pan, for 10 minutes.

2 Heat the oil in a large frying pan or wok and add the onions and potatoes. Fry for 2 minutes.

3 Add the garam masala and nutmeg and fry for 1 minute.

4 Add the mushrooms and fry for 1 minute.

5 Add the rest of the ingredients, apart from the coriander. Season well with salt and pepper. Simmer for 8 minutes.

6 Serve with the rice and garnish with coriander.

RDA 100%

501kcal	13g	26g	13g	73g	10g	7g	1g
CALORIES	PROTEIN	FAT	SAT FAT	CARBS	SUGAR	FIBRE	SALT

BOMBAY POTATOES WITH ROGAN JOSH CURRY

The aim with the Bombay potatoes was to keep things as simple as possible whilst still delivering on some big flavours.

BOMBAY POTATOES

2 tablespoons **olive oil**

1 teaspoon **mustard seeds**

½ teaspoon **mild chilli powder**

½ teaspoon **turmeric**

4 medium **potatoes**, cut into chunks

2 **spring onions**, finely sliced

CURRY

2 tablespoons **olive oil**

1 **onion**, sliced

2 **carrots**, diced

400g tin **green lentils**, drained and rinsed

6 **tomatoes**, chopped

2 **parsnips**, chopped

2 **sweet potatoes**, cut into chunks

3 tablespoons **Rogan Josh curry paste**

1 mug (300ml) **water**

1 Preheat the oven to 180°C fan/200°C/gas 6. Grease a casserole dish.

2 Heat the oil in a frying pan, add the spices and fry for 1 minute. Add the potatoes, season with salt and pepper, and mix.

3 Pour onto a roasting tray and bake in the oven for 25 minutes. Once out of the oven, add the spring onions.

4 Meanwhile, make the curry. Heat the oil in a large saucepan or wok. Add the onions and fry for 2–3 minutes until they soften.

5 Add the rest of the ingredients and bring to the boil. Season well with salt and pepper. Simmer, with a lid on the pan, for 15–20 minutes, or until all the vegetables are cooked through.

6 Serve with the potatoes.

RDA 100%

591kcal	11g	19g	3g	86g	22g	15g	1g
CALORIES	PROTEIN	FAT	SAT FAT	CARBS	SUGAR	FIBRE	SALT

OYSTER MUSHROOMS AND CASHEW STIR-FRY

Quick and easy to make. The crunchy cashews are a delight.

VEGAN OPTION: use maple syrup instead of honey.

GLUTEN-FREE OPTION: use GF soy sauce.

1 ½ mugs (375g) **basmati rice**

2 **pak choi**, sliced

1 mug (200g) **cashew nuts**

2 tablespoons **toasted sesame oil**

1 **red onion**, sliced

2 cloves **garlic**, chopped

2 tablespoons freshly grated **ginger**

1 **fat red chilli**, chopped

1 **red pepper**, sliced

250g **oyster mushrooms**, chopped

SAUCE

3 tablespoons **mirin rice wine vinegar**

3 tablespoons **soy sauce**

2 tablespoons **honey**

1 mug (300ml) **water**

1 tablespoon **cornflour**

1 Put the rice in a pan with 3 mugs of boiling water. Bring to the boil and simmer gently, with a lid on the pan, for 8 minutes.

2 Add the pak choi to the pan and return the lid. Remove from the heat and set to one side.

3 Meanwhile, put the cashews in a dry wok and dry-fry them for 3–4 minutes, stirring frequently. They should get lightly browned. Remove them from the pan and set to one side until needed.

4 Add the oil to the wok and add the onions, garlic, ginger, chilli and peppers. Fry for 2–3 minutes.

5 Add the mushrooms and fry for 1 minute.

6 Mix together the sauce ingredients and add to the wok. Bring to the boil and simmer for 1 minute.

7 Stir the pak choi into the rice and share among the bowls and sprinkle over the cashews.

RDA 100%

584kcal	18g	31g	6g	77g	22g	5g	2g
CALORIES	PROTEIN	FAT	SAT FAT	CARBS	SUGAR	FIBRE	SALT

POLENTA WITH BORLOTTI BEAN STEW

Real comfort food. Great winter warmer with the rich, cheesey polenta and stew.

GLUTEN-FREE OPTION: use GF flour and stock cubes.

1 mug (200g) **fine polenta**

4 mugs (1200ml) **water**

2 **veg stock cubes**

³/₄ mug (45g) grated **Parmesan-style cheese**

2 tablespoons freshly chopped **basil**

2 tablespoons **olive oil**

2 **onions**, sliced

250g **mushrooms**, sliced

1 tablespoon **plain flour**

400g tin **borlotti beans**, drained and rinsed

1 mug (300ml) **water**

1 **veg stock cube**

1 tablespoon **maple syrup**

1 tablespoon **balsamic vinegar**

1 **fat red chilli**, chopped

1 Put the polenta, water and stock in a large saucepan and bring to the boil. Simmer for 10 minutes, stirring constantly. Add the Parmesan and basil and mix. Set to one side until needed.

2 To make the stew, heat the oil in a large frying pan and fry the onions on medium heat until they are quite brown.

3 Add the mushrooms and fry for 2 minutes.

4 Add the flour and season well with salt and pepper. Mix together.

5 Add the rest of the ingredients and bring to the boil. Simmer for 2–3 minutes.

6 Serve the stew over the polenta.

RDA 100%

| 420kcal | 8g | 11g | 3g | 65g | 9g | 9g | 1g |
| CALORIES | PROTEIN | FAT | SAT FAT | CARBS | SUGAR | FIBRE | SALT |

PISTACHIO PESTO PASTA BAKE

Good luck saying this title fast, over and over again. Go on, try it!

GLUTEN-FREE OPTION: use GF pasta.

3 mugs **pasta**

PESTO
²/₃ mug (100g) **pistachios**

100g **basil**

2 tablespoons **extra virgin olive oil**

salt and **pepper**

1 tablespoon **olive oil**

1 **onion**, sliced

250g **mushrooms**, chopped

300g **cherry tomatoes**

150g **vegetarian goat's cheese**, sliced

1   Put the pasta in a pan of boiling, salted water and simmer for 10 minutes. Retain ¹/₂ mug of the cooking liquid. Drain and return to the pan.

2   Meanwhile, put the pesto ingredients in a blender and blitz until fairly smooth, but still with some texture. Add the ¹/₂ mug of pasta liquid. Set to one side until needed.

3   Preheat the grill.

4   Heat the oil in a frying pan and fry the onions until they begin to brown.

5   Add the mushrooms and fry for 2 minutes.

6   Add the tomatoes and fry for 1 minute.

7   Add the pesto to the drained pasta and mix. Transfer to a greased casserole dish.

8   Put the contents of the frying pan on top.

9   Top with the sliced, goat's cheese and place under the grill until the cheese browns.

RDA 100%

546kcal	19g	33g	11g	41g	8g	15g	3g
CALORIES	PROTEIN	FAT	SAT FAT	CARBS	SUGAR	FIBRE	SALT

GREEN LENTIL AND TOMATO SPAGHETTI

Really quick dish, you end up pretty much cooking everything in the time it takes to cook the spaghetti.

GLUTEN-FREE OPTION: use GF stock cubes and spaghetti.

400g **spaghetti**

2 tablespoons **olive oil**

1 **red onion**, chopped

2 cloves **garlic**, chopped

250g **mushrooms**, chopped

400g **cherry tomatoes**, halved

2 tablespoons freshly chopped **basil**

400g tin **green lentils**, drained and rinsed

6 **sun-dried tomatoes**, chopped

2 tablespoons **tomato purée**

1 **veg stock cube**

1 Put the spaghetti in a large pan of boiling, salted water and simmer for 10 minutes. Drain and return to the pan.

2 Meanwhile, heat the oil in a large frying pan and add the onions and garlic. Fry until the onions begin to brown.

3 Add the mushrooms and fry for 1 minute.

4 Add the tomatoes and fry for 1 minute.

5 Add the rest of the ingredients, together with ½ mug (150ml) water, and bring to the boil. Season well with salt and pepper and simmer for 3 minutes.

6 Mix in the cooked spaghetti and serve.

RDA 100%

377kcal	10g	12g	2g	53g	9g	9g	1g
CALORIES	PROTEIN	FAT	SAT FAT	CARBS	SUGAR	FIBRE	SALT

BEAN 'BURGERS' AND POLENTA CHIPS

VEGAN OPTION: use vegan margarine instead of butter in the peas.

GLUTEN-FREE OPTION: use GF bread, soy and stock cubes.

1 mug (200g) **coarse polenta**

4 mugs (1200ml) boiling **water**

3 **veg stock cubes**

2 tablespoons **olive oil**

BURGER

3 slices **bread**

1 **red onion**, chopped

2 cloves **garlic**, chopped

250g **mushrooms**, roughly chopped

400g tin **borlotti beans**, rinsed and drained

1 **fat red chilli**, chopped

2 tablespoons **tomato purée**

1 tablespoon **soy sauce**

2 tablespoons **miso paste**

2 tablespoons **olive oil**

3 mugs (450g) **frozen peas**, defrosted

25g **butter**, measure using packet

1 Put the water, polenta and stock cubes in a large saucepan. Simmer for 10 minutes, stirring constantly. Tip out into a greased traybake tin and leave to set for 2 hours.

2 Once the polenta is set, preheat the oven to 180°C fan/200°C/gas 6.

3 Cut the polenta into 'chips' and place on a large roasting tray. Drizzle with oil and mix everything together. Spread out and roast in the oven for 45–50 minutes.

4 Meanwhile, put the bread in a food processor and make into breadcrumbs. Add the onions, garlic and mushrooms and pulse a few times. Don't make things too fine.

5 Remove from the processor and place in a large bowl. Add the rest of the burger ingredients to the processor and pulse a few times. Add to the bowl, season well with salt and pepper, and mix.

6 Heat the oil in a frying pan and add spoonfuls of the mixture. Fry gently until browned on both sides.

7 Put the peas in a pan of boiling water and simmer for 1 minute. Drain and return to the pan with the butter. Mash.

RDA 100%

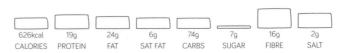

| 626kcal | 19g | 24g | 6g | 74g | 7g | 16g | 2g |
| CALORIES | PROTEIN | FAT | SAT FAT | CARBS | SUGAR | FIBRE | SALT |

£1.46 /PERSON | SERVES 4 | EASE ★★★☆☆ | PREP 25 MINS | COOK 45 MINS | GF OPTION

PEA AND FETA FRITTERS

The pickled cucumbers in the salad make a real difference. Try them in other salads too.

GLUTEN-FREE OPTION: use GF flour.

5 medium **potatoes**, cut into small chunks

2 **sweet potatoes**, peeled and cut into small chunks

2 tablespoons **olive oil**

FRITTERS

4 mugs (600g) **frozen peas**, defrosted

200g **feta cheese**, crumbled

3 **eggs**, beaten

½ mug (100g) **self-raising flour**

2 tablespoons freshly chopped **mint**

2 tablespoons **olive oil**

SALAD

1 bunch **spring onions**, sliced lengthways

4 **pickled cucumbers**, sliced

2 **Little Gem lettuce**, sliced

1 **fat red chilli**, sliced

DRESSING

2 tablespoons **extra virgin olive oil**

2 tablespoons **honey**

2 tablespoons **cider vinegar**

1 Preheat the oven to 180°C fan/200°C/gas 6. Put the potatoes and sweet potatoes on a roasting tray. Drizzle with oil and season with salt and pepper. Mix together and then spread out. Roast in the oven for 45 minutes.

2 Mix together the fritter ingredients in a large bowl. Season well with salt and pepper.

3 Heat the oil in a frying pan and add small piles of the mixture. Fry on a medium heat until nicely browned on both sides.

4 Mix together the salad ingredients and season with salt and pepper. Mix with the combined dressing ingredients.

RDA 100%

998kcal	35g	41g	14g	114g	25g	18g	2g
CALORIES	PROTEIN	FAT	SAT FAT	CARBS	SUGAR	FIBRE	SALT

£ 1.76 /PERSON | SERVES 4 | EASE ★★★★★ | PREP 25 MINS | COOK 20 MINS

JACKFRUIT STEW WITH YORKSHIRE PUDS

Jackfruit is a really versatile ingredient, the longer you cook it the more is softens and starts to pull apart which is really nice.

YORKSHIRE PUDS

12 teaspoons **rapeseed oil**

4 large **eggs**

120g **plain flour**

70ml **milk**

30ml **water**

JACKFRUIT STEW

3 tablespoons **rapeseed oil**

1 **red onion**, sliced

2 cloves **garlic**, chopped

250g **mushrooms**, sliced

1 tin **jackfruit**, drained, rinsed and chopped

1 tablespoon **plain flour**

400g tin **green lentils**, drained and rinsed

3 tablespoons **pomegranate molasses**

1 ½ mugs (450ml) **water**

1 **veg stock cube**

100g **kale**

1 Preheat the oven 250°C fan/270°C/gas 9.

2 Put 1 teaspoon of rapeseed oil in each hole of a 12 hole bun tin. Place in the oven to heat up.

3 Beat together the eggs and flour. Add the milk and water and beat well.

4 Once the oil in the tin is nice and hot, pour the pudding mix into the individual holes. Place in the oven for 20 minutes. They should be risen and nicely browned.

5 Meanwhile, make the jackfruit stew. Heat the oil in a frying pan and add the onions. Fry for 2–3 minutes until they begin to soften. Season well.

6 Add the garlic and mushrooms and fry for a further 2 minutes.

7 Add the jackfruit and fry for 2 minutes.

8 Add the rest of the ingredients and simmer for 8–10 minutes.

9 Meanwhile, put the kale in a wok with 2 tablespoons of water and a tablespoon of rapeseed oil. Simmer gently, with a lid on the pan, for 2 minutes.

10 Serve on the Yorkshire pud with the kale.

RDA 100%

| 628kcal | 20g | 33g | 4g | 61g | 10g | 12g | 1g |
| CALORIES | PROTEIN | FAT | SAT FAT | CARBS | SUGAR | FIBRE | SALT |

CASHEW HOISIN STIR-FRY

One of those simple, speedy dishes that is packed with flavour and with a lovely, crunchy texture.

GLUTEN-FREE OPTION: use GF hoisin sauce.

1 ½ mugs (375g) **basmati rice**

2 tablespoons **toasted sesame oil**

250g **chestnut mushrooms**, sliced

1 bunch **spring onions**, chopped

175g **baby sweetcorn**, halved lengthways

2 cloves **garlic**, chopped

2 **fat red chillies**, deseeded and chopped

100g **sugar snaps**, halved lengthways

½ mug (100g) **cashew nuts**

240ml jar **hoisin sauce**

1 Put the rice in a saucepan with 3 mugs of boiling water. Bring to the boil and simmer gently, with a lid on the pan, for 10 minutes.

2 Meanwhile, heat the oil in a wok, or large frying pan. Add the mushrooms, spring onions, sweetcorn and garlic and fry for 2–3 minutes.

3 Add the chillies, sugar snaps and cashews and fry for another 1 minute.

4 Add the hoisin to the wok. Bring to the boil and then simmer for 1 minute.

5 Serve with the rice.

RDA 100%

469kcal	15g	22g	4g	76g	26g	6g	2g
CALORIES	PROTEIN	FAT	SAT FAT	CARBS	SUGAR	FIBRE	SALT

HALLOUMI WITH CAULIFLOWER COUSCOUS

The chilli sauce that tops this dish certainly packs a punch. You can use only one chilli if you don't fancy that much heat.

CHILLI SAUCE

½ mug (150ml) **cold water**

2 tablespoons **sun-dried tomato purée**

2 tablespoons **honey**

2 **fat red chillies**, chopped

1 tablespoon **cornflour**

1 tablespoon **olive oil**

2 blocks **halloumi**, sliced

2 tablespoons **olive oil**

1 **cauliflower**, cut into florets

2 mugs (300g) **frozen peas**, defrosted

1 bunch **spring onions**, chopped

2 tablespoons freshly chopped **mint**

1 Mix together the sauce ingredients, put in a small pan and then bring to the boil. The sauce should thicken. Set aside until needed.

2 Heat the oil in a frying pan and add the halloumi. Fry on each side until browned. Set aside until needed.

3 Put the cauliflower in a food processor and blitz, until they look like breadcrumbs. If you don't have a processor, just chop very finely.

4 Heat the 2 tablespoons of olive oil in the frying pan. Add the cauliflower and fry for 2–3 minutes. Once the cauliflower begins to steam, it is cooked.

5 Add the peas, spring onions and mint and stir together. Season well with salt and pepper.

6 Cut the fried halloumi into strips and serve on top of the couscous, with the sauce.

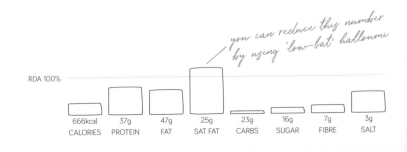

you can reduce this number by using 'low-fat' halloumi

RDA 100%

| 666kcal CALORIES | 37g PROTEIN | 47g FAT | 25g SAT FAT | 23g CARBS | 16g SUGAR | 7g FIBRE | 3g SALT |

STUFFED PEPPERS WITH LYONNAISE POTATOES

Tim is not normally a fan of stuffed peppers, as the flavour can sometimes not match the amount of effort it takes to stuff them. These ones made the cut, so they must deliver on flavour!

5 medium **potatoes**, sliced

2 **onions**, sliced

2 cloves **garlic**, sliced

2 tablespoons **olive oil**

2 **red peppers**

2 **yellow peppers**

285g **firm tofu**, chopped

1 **red onion**, chopped

400g tin **green lentils**, drained and rinsed

12 **black olives**, roughly chopped

125g **chestnut mushrooms**, chopped

5 **sun-dried tomatoes**, chopped

1 Preheat the oven to 200°C fan/220°C/gas 7.

2 Layer the potatoes, onions and garlic in a roasting tray. Season with salt and pepper. Drizzle over the oil. Bake in the oven for 50 minutes, or until nicely browned.

3 Cut the peppers in half, horizontally and remove the seeds and veins.

4 Mix together the tofu, onions, lentils, olives, mushrooms and sundried tomatoes. Season with salt and pepper.

5 Stuff the peppers with the mixture and drizzle a little oil on top.

6 Place on a baking tray and bake in the oven for 40 minutes.

RDA 100%

541kcal	21g	16g	3g	73g	22g	14g	1g
CALORIES	PROTEIN	FAT	SAT FAT	CARBS	SUGAR	FIBRE	SALT

PERSIAN POLENTA CAKE

The orange glaze and chopped up pistachios add a lovely sticky and crunchy topping.

GLUTEN-FREE OPTION: use GF baking powder.

200g **butter**

300g **coconut sugar**

5 **eggs**

150g **pistachios**, roughly chopped

zest of 2 **oranges**

250g **ground almonds**

200g **polenta**

1 teaspoon **baking powder**

juice of 2 **oranges**

4 tablespoons **coconut sugar**

30g **pistachios**, chopped

1 Preheat the oven to 160°C fan/180°C/gas 5. Grease and line a 23cm loose-bottomed cake tin.

2 In a mixing bowl, beat the butter and sugar together.

3 Add the eggs, one at a time, beating well between each addition.

4 Add the 150g of pistachios and orange zest and stir together.

5 Mix the ground almonds, polenta and baking powder and add to the mixture, folding in gently.

6 Pour into the cake tin and smooth out.

7 Bake in the oven for 45 minutes. The cake should bounce back when lightly pressed.

8 While the cake is baking, put the orange juice and coconut sugar in a small saucepan and simmer gently, until the sugar has melted.

9 Take the cake out of the oven and drizzle over the syrup. Sprinkle with the remaining pistachios.

RDA 100%

571kcal	13g	35g	11g	50g	33g	9g	2g
CALORIES	PROTEIN	FAT	SAT FAT	CARBS	SUGAR	FIBRE	SALT

 £0.32 /PERSON
 SERVES 12
 EASE ★★★☆☆
 PREP 10 MINS
 COOK 14 MINS
 GF OPTION

ECCLES CAKES

Proper northern cakes, originally from Eccles in Lancashire, filled with sticky fruit with a flaky, puffed pastry.

GLUTEN-FREE OPTION: use GF pastry.

FILLING

40g **butter**

75g **raisins**

75g **soft brown sugar**

40g **mixed peel**

zest of an **orange**

½ teaspoon **cinnamon**

2 sheets **ready-rolled puff pastry**

1 tablespoon **granulated sugar**

1 **egg**, beaten

1 Preheat the oven to 200°C fan/220°C/gas 7.

2 Line 2 baking trays.

3 Melt the butter in a small saucepan and add the rest of the filling ingredients. Mix together, don't heat.

4 Unroll the pastry and cut into 12 circles (10cm diameter). Place a blob of the filling in the centre of each one. Fold up the edges and form into a round.

5 Place on the sheets, messy side down, and squash a little.

6 Make 2 cuts on the top of each cake. Brush with the beaten egg and sprinkle with sugar.

7 Bake in the oven for 12–14 minutes, until nicely golden and crisp.

RDA 100%

324kcal	4g	18g	10g	36g	10g	1g	0.5g
CALORIES	PROTEIN	FAT	SAT FAT	CARBS	SUGAR	FIBRE	SALT

ALMOND AND PUMPKIN FLAPJACKS

Packed with energy. Perfect in a packed lunch to help you power through the day!

GLUTEN-FREE OPTION: use GF oats.

150g **butter**

90g **soft brown sugar**

75g **honey**

100g **medjool dates**, de-stoned and chopped

50g **cashew nut butter** (see p218)

250g **oats**

125g **flaked almonds**

50g **pumpkin seeds**

1 Preheat the oven to 160°C fan/180°C/gas 5.

2 Line a 20 x 30cm cake tin.

3 Put the butter, sugar, honey and medjool dates in a large saucepan. Gently heat until the sugar melts. Whisk in the nut butter until it is smooth.

4 Add the oats, almonds and pumpkin seeds. Mix well.

5 Press into the tin and bake in the oven for 25 minutes.

6 Once cooled, cut into slices.

RDA 100%

356kcal	7g	22g	8g	32g	18g	3g	0.2g
CALORIES	PROTEIN	FAT	SAT FAT	CARBS	SUGAR	FIBRE	SALT

LAVENDER AND HONEY CAKE

Dried lavender can be found with the dried herbs and spices. If you can't find any, don't worry, this cake still tastes amazing without it. It is still worth having a look though.

GLUTEN-FREE OPTION: use GF flour and baking powder + ½ teaspoon xanthan gum.

CAKE

225g **butter**

100g **caster sugar**

3 **eggs**

75g **honey**

zest of 2 **lemons**

1 teaspoon **vanilla bean paste**

2 teaspoons **dried lavender**

225g **ground almonds**

110g **self-raising flour**

1 teaspoon **baking powder**

3 tablespoons **lemon curd**

juice of a **lemon**

2 tablespoons **granulated sugar**

crème fraîche

1 Preheat the oven to 160°C fan/180°C/gas 5. Grease and line 2 x 20cm round cake tins.

2 Beat together the butter and sugar.

3 Add the eggs, one at a time, beating well between each addition.

4 Add the honey, lemon zest and vanilla bean paste and beat well.

5 Add the rest of the cake ingredients and fold in gently.

6 Pour half into each tin and smooth out evenly.

7 Bake in the oven for 30 minutes.

8 Once the cake is cooked, leave to cool for about 20 minutes.

9 Spread one cake with the lemon curd and sandwich the other cake on top. Mix together the lemon juice and sugar and pour over the top.

10 Serve with crème fraîche.

RDA 100%

531kcal CALORIES | 10g PROTEIN | 39g FAT | 17g SAT FAT | 33g CARBS | 25g SUGAR | 2g FIBRE | 1g SALT

BEETROOT CHOCOLATE CAKE

Have fun when spreading out the ganache. Making little indents with the side of a knife, or scoring with a fork, can make this cake look really interesting.

GLUTEN-FREE OPTION: use GF baking powder.

250g **cooked beetroot**

4 **eggs**

1 teaspoon **vanilla extract**

5 tablespoons **honey**

125g **dark chocolate**

4 tablespoons **light olive oil**

125g **ground almonds**

1 teaspoon **baking powder**

1 tablespoon **cocoa powder**

CHOCOLATE GANACHE

150ml **double cream**

150g **dark chocolate**

1 Preheat the oven to 160°C fan/180°C/gas 5.

2 Grease and line a 23cm springform tin.

3 Blitz the beetroot with a blender until smooth. Add to a mixing bowl, along with the eggs, vanilla and honey. Beat with a food mixer, until it is pale and thickens a little.

4 Melt the chocolate in a bowl over a pan of simmering water. Add to the mixing bowl with the olive oil.

5 Mix the almonds, baking powder and cocoa and add to the mixture, folding in gently.

6 Pour into the tin and level out.

7 Bake in the oven for 45 minutes.

8 To make the chocolate ganache, gently bring the cream to the boil. Take off the heat and add the chocolate. Stir until it melts. Transfer to a bowl and leave to cool in the fridge.

9 Once the cake has cooked and cooled, the ganache should be thick enough to spread on the top.

RDA 100%

361kcal	9g	28g	11g	19g	17g	4g	0.2g
CALORIES	PROTEIN	FAT	SAT FAT	CARBS	SUGAR	FIBRE	SALT

£0.80 /PERSON | SERVES 8 | EASE ★★☆☆☆ | PREP 15 MINS | 20 MINS FREEZING | GF

ICE CREAM SUNDAES

When you get a good mouthfull of all three elements of these sundaes, it is a real winner. If you don't use all the coconut flakes, they will keep well for a few weeks in a sealed jar.

COCONUT CRISPS

2 tablespoons **maple syrup**

1 tablespoon **coconut oil**

1 tablespoon **honey**

3 mugs (150g) **flaked coconut chips**

BLUEBERRY ICE CREAM

2 mugs (300g) **frozen blueberries**

½ mug (150ml) **double cream**

1 tablespoon **honey**

STRAWBERRY ICE CREAM

2 mugs (300g) **frozen strawberries**

½ mug (150ml) **double cream**

1 tablespoon **honey**

1 Preheat the oven to 170°C fan/190°C/gas 5.

2 Put the maple syrup, coconut oil and honey in a medium saucepan and gently heat. Add the coconut flakes and mix.

3 Put a silicone sheet on a baking tray. Spread the coconut mix over the tray.

4 Bake in the oven for 10 minutes. Take out of the oven and mix everything around to expose more coconut to the heat. Return to the oven for a further 5 minutes. Leave to cool.

5 To make the ice creams, put the frozen blueberries in a food processor and blitz. Add the cream and honey and blitz again. Put into a plastic box and leave in the freezer for 20 minutes. Repeat the process with the strawberries.

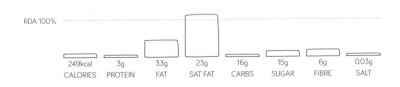

RDA 100%

| 249kcal | 3g | 33g | 23g | 16g | 15g | 6g | 0.03g |
| CALORIES | PROTEIN | FAT | SAT FAT | CARBS | SUGAR | FIBRE | SALT |

MANGO AND COCONUT RICE PUDDING

Only 5 ingredients and amazing. Subtle, creamy, sweetness of coconut-infused rice, with the freshness of the mango, topped with a little treat of crunchy pistachios.

400ml tin **coconut milk**

²/₃ mug (150g) **arborio rice**

1 **mango**, cut into small chunks

2 tablespoons **honey**

25g **pistachios**, chopped

1 Put the coconut milk and rice in a saucepan and bring to the boil. Simmer very gently, with a lid on the pan, for 20 minutes. Check every now and then and stir to make sure it isn't sticking.

2 Put the mango and honey in a frying pan and gently fry for 3 minutes.

3 Serve the mango on top of the pudding and sprinkle over the nuts.

RDA 100%

379kcal	6g	19g	13g	48g	19g	5g	1g
CALORIES	PROTEIN	FAT	SAT FAT	CARBS	SUGAR	FIBRE	SALT

£0.97 /PERSON · SERVES 6 · EASE ★★★☆☆ · PREP 20 MINS · COOK 12 MINS · GF OPTION

SESAME BISCUITS WITH FRIED PINEAPPLE

You can make the biscuits ahead of time, so you are ready to simply fry up the pineapple when you want to serve up.

GLUTEN-FREE OPTION: use GF flour and ¼ teaspoon xanthan gum.

SESAME BISCUITS

20g softened **butter**

75g **coconut sugar**

1 **egg**

1 teaspoon **vanilla bean paste**

45g **pistachios**, roughly chopped

45g **cashew nuts**, roughly chopped

50g **sesame seeds**

75g **plain flour**

2 tablespoons **coconut oil**

1 **whole fresh pineapple**, peeled and cut into slices

2 tablespoons **maple syrup**

300ml **double cream**

zest and juice of a **lime**

1 Preheat the oven to 160°C fan/180°C/gas 4.

2 Grease and line 2 baking sheets.

3 Beat together the butter and sugar. Add the egg and beat well.

4 Add the rest of the biscuit ingredients and fold in.

5 Place teaspoons of the mixture on the baking sheets and bake in the oven for 12 minutes.

6 Heat the coconut oil in a large frying pan. Add the pineapple and maple syrup and fry gently until things begin to brown.

7 Whip the cream and stir in the lime zest and juice.

8 Serve.

198

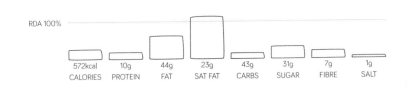

RDA 100%

| 572kcal | 10g | 44g | 23g | 43g | 31g | 7g | 1g |
| CALORIES | PROTEIN | FAT | SAT FAT | CARBS | SUGAR | FIBRE | SALT |

CRÈME BRÛLÉE

We tried these over and over again to get them right (tough life right!?), but we finally settled on this method, which keeps things as simple as possible. Well worth the effort. You can also make these ahead of time and just leave the grilling of the caster sugar when you want to serve them.

600ml **double cream**

6 **egg yolks**

3 tablespoons **caster sugar**

1 teaspoon **vanilla extract**

3 tablespoons **caster sugar**

1 Preheat the oven to 150°C fan/170°C/gas 3.

2 Put the cream in a small saucepan and gently bring almost to the boil.

3 In a large bowl, whisk together egg yolks, sugar, and vanilla. Add the cream and beat until smooth.

4 Pour into 6 ramekins and place them in a deep roasting tray.

5 Put the tray on the middle shelf of the oven and then add boiling water around the ramekins, so it comes ½ way up the sides. Bake for 40 minutes.

6 Leave to cool for about 1 hour.

7 Preheat the grill to the hottest it will go! Sprinkle the rest of the caster sugar over the tops of the ramekins and then place them under the grill for 2–3 minutes, until the sugar begins to bubble and brown. Keep a close eye on them, so they don't burn.

8 Serve either hot or cold.

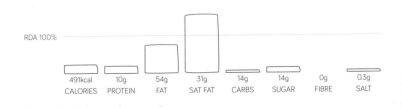

RDA 100%							
491kcal	10g	54g	31g	14g	14g	0g	0.3g
CALORIES	PROTEIN	FAT	SAT FAT	CARBS	SUGAR	FIBRE	SALT

LEMON POSSET WITH BUTTER SHORTBREAD

There is something quite decadent about ignoring your spoon and just dipping shortbread biscuits into a lemon posset!

GLUTEN-FREE OPTION: use GF flour + ½ teaspoon xanthan gum.

125g **butter**
150g **caster sugar**
1 **egg**
125g **self-raising flour**
100g **ground almonds**
600ml **double cream**
150ml **maple syrup**
2 **lemons**, zest and juice
300g **strawberries**

1 Preheat the oven to 180°C fan/200°C/gas 6. Grease and line a baking tray.

2 Beat together the butter and sugar. Add the egg and beat well. Add the flour and ground almonds and mix together.

3 Roll into about 20 balls. Place on the baking tray and squash down with a fork.

4 Bake in the oven for 12-15 minutes.

5 To make the posset, put the cream and syrup in a saucepan and bring to the boil. Whisk in the lemon zest and juice.

6 Divide amongst 6 bowls and place in the fridge to set for around 1-2 hours.

7 Serve with the strawberries and the shortbread biscuits.

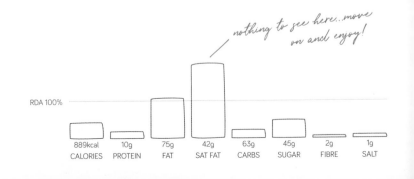

nothing to see here...move on and enjoy!

RDA 100%

| 889kcal | 10g | 75g | 42g | 63g | 45g | 2g | 1g |
| CALORIES | PROTEIN | FAT | SAT FAT | CARBS | SUGAR | FIBRE | SALT |

BAKED PEARS

Tim hates baked pears! So getting anything that even resembles a baked pear past him is a tall order. Against all odds this one got through with no problems at all. Tender, fluffy and juicy. No complaints, only empty plates!

zest and juice of an **orange**

1 mug (300ml) **apple juice**

½ mug (100g) **coconut sugar** or **soft brown sugar**

1 **cinnamon stick**

4 **Williams pears**, peeled

50g **butter**, measure using packet

300ml **crème fraîche**

1 Preheat the oven to 170°C fan/190°C/gas 5.

2 Put the orange juice, zest, apple juice, sugar and cinnamon stick in a saucepan. Bring to the boil and simmer for 5–10 minutes.

3 Transfer to a casserole dish and add the pears. Bake in the oven for 45 minutes. Baste once during the cooking period.

4 Once cooked, remove the pears from the liquid and place in bowls ready to serve. Pour the liquid back into a saucepan and add the butter to the pan. Mix. Boil briskly for 2–3 minutes to reduce the liquid. Add to the pears in the serving dishes, along with a dollop of crème fraîche.

RDA 100%

| 459kcal | 2g | 34g | 23g | 36g | 35g | 1g | 0.3g |
| CALORIES | PROTEIN | FAT | SAT FAT | CARBS | SUGAR | FIBRE | SALT |

£ 0.72 /PERSON · SERVES 6 · EASE ★★★★☆ · PREP 25 MINS · COOK 60 MINS · GF

CHOCOLATE ORANGE AND ALMOND PAVLOVA

What a treat, crunchy on the outside and soft and chewy on the inside. Perfect.

4 **egg whites**
240g **caster sugar**
50g **ground almonds**

CHOCOLATE SAUCE
50g **butter**
100g **dark chocolate**
2 tablespoons **light brown sugar**
4 tablespoons **double cream**

300ml **double cream**
3 **oranges**, segmented

1 Preheat the oven to 150°C fan/170°C/gas 3. Line a large baking tray.

2 Beat the egg whites until stiff.

3 Gradually add the caster sugar and beat well until silky. Using a food-mixer here is pretty helpful.

4 Carefully fold in the ground almonds. Pour the mixture onto the baking tray and form into a round.

5 Bake in the oven for 1 hour. Turn the oven off and leave the Pavlova in the oven for a further 15 minutes. Take out.

6 Make the chocolate sauce. Put the chocolate sauce ingredients in a small saucepan and gently heat until the sugar is melted. Leave to cool.

7 Beat the cream until it thickens, and when the Pavlova is cooled, spread the cream on top.

8 Arrange the oranges on top.

9 Once the sauce has cooled, drizzle over the top of the Pavlova.

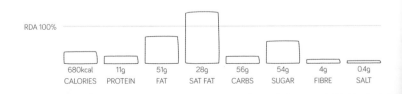

RDA 100%

| 680kcal | 11g | 51g | 28g | 56g | 54g | 4g | 0.4g |
| CALORIES | PROTEIN | FAT | SAT FAT | CARBS | SUGAR | FIBRE | SALT |

 £1.04 /PERSON
 SERVES 6
 EASE ★★★★☆
 PREP 25 MINS
 COOK 25 MINS
 GF OPTION

TART TATIN WITH HOMEMADE CUSTARD

You need an ovenproof frying pan for this. Check yours is OK in the oven before you melt the handle!

GLUTEN-FREE OPTION: use GF pastry.

50g **butter**, measure using packet

100g **soft brown sugar**

5 **Pink Lady apples**, cored and sliced

320g pack **ready-rolled puff pastry**

beaten **egg** to brush

600ml **double cream**

6 **egg yolks**

50g **caster sugar**

1 teaspoon **vanilla bean paste**

1 Preheat the oven to 200°C fan/220°C/gas 7.

2 Heat the butter in an ovenproof frying pan. Add the sugar and cook for one minute. Add the apples to the pan and fry for 2–3 minutes, taking care not to burn the sugar. Remove from the heat.

3 Place the pastry over the top and trim off any excess. Brush with the beaten egg.

4 Bake in the oven for 20–25 minutes.

5 Meanwhile, put the cream in a saucepan and bring to the boil.

6 In a mixing bowl, beat together the egg yolks, sugar and vanilla bean paste. Pour the cream over and stir well.

7 Put back in the saucepan and heat gently until the custard thickens a little (it will, however, still remain fairly thin).

this custard is very creamy, after all!

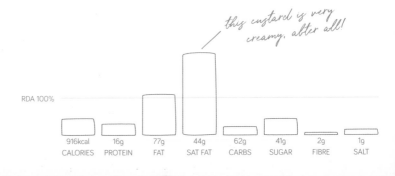

RDA 100%

916kcal	16g	77g	44g	62g	41g	2g	1g
CALORIES	PROTEIN	FAT	SAT FAT	CARBS	SUGAR	FIBRE	SALT

PISTACHIO AND RASPBERRY CHEESECAKE

Wow, I mean, just look at the colour of this cheesecake! The contrast of the freeze-dried rasperries and the green of the pistachios was always going to be a winner.

WHERE ON EARTH: Freeze-dried raspberries are in the supermarket 'baking section'.

75g **flaked coconut chips**

130g **whole almonds**

50g **medjool dates**, de-stoned

65g **butter**, melted

300ml **double cream**

280g **Philadelphia cream cheese**

zest and juice of 3 **limes**

2 teaspoons **vanilla bean paste**

3 tablespoons **icing sugar**

50g **pistachios**, finely chopped

5g **freeze-dried raspberries**, crushed slightly

1 Put the flaked coconut chips, almonds and medjool dates in a food processor and blitz. Add the melted butter and pulse a few times.

2 Grease and line a 20cm loose-bottomed cake tin. Press the nut mixture into the bottom.

3 Beat the cream until it is stiff.

4 Add the Philadelphia, lime zest and juice, vanilla bean paste and icing sugar. Mix together.

5 Spread the mixture over the nut base in the tin and smooth out.

6 Leave in the fridge for at least 2 hours to set.

7 Sprinkle the pistachios and freeze-dried raspberries over the top.

RDA 100%

| 360kcal CALORIES | 8g PROTEIN | 40g FAT | 21g SAT FAT | 11g CARBS | 9g SUGAR | 5g FIBRE | 1g SALT |

PEANUT BUTTER

CHILLI JAM

CHILLI SAUCE

SALSA VERDE

COCONUT CRISPS

PICKLED BEETROOT

SALSA VERDE

2 cloves **garlic**

25g **fresh parsley**

50g **fresh basil**

25g **fresh mint**

2 tablespoons **capers**

3 **pickled gherkins**

2 teaspoons **Dijon mustard**

3 tablespoons **wine vinegar**

8 tablespoons **extra virgin olive oil**

1 Put everything in a blender and blitz until smooth.

2 Store in a sterilised, airtight jar in the fridge.

BEETROOT PICKLE

3 large **raw beetroots**, peeled and cut into thin strips, or grated

2 tablespoons **cider vinegar**

1 tablespoon **coconut sugar**

1 Mix together and store in a sterilised, airtight jar in the fridge.

COCONUT CRISPS

4 tablespoons **soy sauce**

2 tablespoons **maple syrup**

1 teaspoon **paprika**

3 mugs (150g) **flaked coconut chips**

1 Preheat the oven to 170°C fan/190°C/gas 5.

2 Mix everything together in a large bowl.

3 Spread the mixture out over a large, greased baking tray.

4 Bake in the oven for 10 minutes. Take out of the oven and stir. Bake in the oven for a further 10 minutes.

5 Allow to cool and then store in sterilised, airtight jars.

CHILLI JAM

1 tablespoon **rapeseed oil**

3 **fat red chillies**, chopped

2 tablespoons freshly grated **ginger**

½ mug (150ml) **cider vinegar**

½ mug (150ml) **water**

¾ mug (150g) **coconut sugar**

2 tablespoons **cornflour**

2 tablespoons **water**

1 Heat the oil in a frying pan, add the chillies and ginger and fry for 1 minute.

2 Add the cider vinegar, water and coconut sugar and simmer for 2 minutes.

3 Mix together the cornflour and water and add to the pan. Simmer for 2 minutes.

4 Leave to cool slightly and then store in a sterilised, airtight jar in the fridge.

NUT BUTTERS

We have used nut butter in quite a few recipes. It is easy to make if you have a food processor and is much healthier than most bought peanut butters. However, you can find some bought nut butters with no added sugar or salt.

CASHEW NUT BUTTER
2 mugs (400g) **cashew nuts**
4 tablespoons **toasted sesame oil**

HAZELNUT BUTTER
2 mugs (400g) **roasted chopped hazelnuts**
1 tablespoon **toasted sesame oil**

PEANUT BUTTER
2 mugs (400g) **peanuts**
4 tablespoons **toasted sesame oil**

ALMOND BUTTER
2 mugs (400g) **blanched almonds**
4 tablespoons **toasted sesame oil**

1 Put the nuts in a large frying pan and toast gently for 3–4 minutes. Keep them moving to avoid burning.

2 Place in a food processor and blitz for about 5 minutes, until they form a paste. Add the oil and blitz to form a soft paste.

3 Store in a sterilised, airtight jar.

SWEET CHILLI SAUCE

2 tablespoons **cornflour**

1 mug (300ml) **water**

1 tablespoon **red wine vinegar**

2 tablespoons **tomato purée**

3 tablespoons **maple syrup**

2 **fat red chillies**

1 Blitz all the ingredients together and transfer to a small saucepan. Bring to the boil and simmer for one minute.

2 Store in the fridge in a sterilised, airtight glass bottle, or jar.

INDEX

DISCLAIMER

Throughout this book we have tried to alert you to allergens, namely gluten, that could be present in ingredients in the book. However, it is still your responsibility to make sure that the products you buy, and cook with, do not contain any allergens that you, or anyone you are cooking for, will react to. Please carefully read the labels of anything you buy.

Recipe prices are an average of Tesco and Sainsbury's pricing as at JUNE 2019.

Published by: Intrade (GB) Ltd

Contact: us@noshbooks.com

ISBN: 978-0-9567464-3-6

Printed in China

1st Edition: January 2020

Author: Joy May

Editor: Ron May

Photography: Ben May

Food Stylist: Tim May

Design: Milk Bottle Designs

Proof-reading: Fran Maciver

Thanks for your support:

FREE
NOSH MENU
& SHOPPING
APP

Just pick any number of recipes, from any of our books,
and create a menu and shopping list in seconds.